Acting Edition

PETER PAN GOES WRONG

BY HENRY LEWIS, JONATHAN SAYER & HENRY SHIELDS

ISBN 978-0-8222-4574-2
www.dramatists.com
www.concordtheatricals.com

This work is published by Dramatists Play Service, an imprint of Concord Theatricals Corp.

IMPORTANT BILLING AND CREDIT REQUIREMENTS

PETER PAN GOES WRONG was first presented by Mischief Theatre on December 10, 2013, at the Pleasance Theatre in London. It was directed by Adam Meggido, the design was by Martin Thomas, the lighting design was by Owen Evans, the sound design was by Ella Wahlström, the choreography was by Nell Mooney, the composers were Richard Baker and Rob Falconer, and the assistant director was Andy MacNamee. The cast was as follows:

CHRIS ..... Henry Shields
ROBERT ..... Henry Lewis
FRANCIS ..... Harry Kershaw
SANDRA ..... Charlie Russell
DENNIS ..... Jonathan Sayer
ANNIE ..... Sophie Whittaker and Nancy Zamit
MAX ..... Dave Hearn
TREVOR ..... Rob Falconer
JONATHAN ..... Greg Tannahill
LUCY ..... Daisy Waterstone

The production of PETER PAN GOES WRONG was then presented by Kenny Wax Ltd. and Stage Presence Ltd. on a UK national tour in 2014–15. The director was Adam Meggido, the set design was by Simon Scullion, the lighting design was by Matt Haskins, the costume design was by Roberto Surace, the sound design was by Ella Wahlström, the composers were Richard Baker and Rob Falconer, and the assistant director was Sita Thomas. The cast was as follows:

CHRIS ..... Laurence Pears
ROBERT ..... Cornelius Booth
FRANCIS ..... Harry Kershaw
SANDRA ..... Leonie Hill
DENNIS ..... James Marlowe
ANNIE ..... Naomi Sheldon
MAX ..... Matt Cavendish
TREVOR ..... Chris Leask
JONATHAN ..... Alex Bartram
LUCY ..... Rosie Abraham
UNDERSTUDIES ..... Fred Gray and Laura Kirman

The touring production of PETER PAN GOES WRONG transferred to the Apollo Theatre in London's West End for the Christmas 2015–2016 season. It was directed by Adam Meggido, the set design was by Simon Scullion, the lighting design was by Matt Haskins, the costume design was by Roberto Surace, the sound design was by Ella Wahlström, the composers were Richard Baker and Rob Falconer, and the choreographers were Dave Hearn and Nancy Zamit. The cast was as follows:

CHRIS .... Henry Shields
ROBERT .... Henry Lewis
FRANCIS .... Tom Edden
SANDRA .... Charlie Russell
DENNIS .... Jonathan Sayer
ANNIE .... Nancy Zamit
MAX .... Dave Hearn
TREVOR .... Chris Leask
JONATHAN .... Greg Tannahill
LUCY .... Ellie Morris
UNDERSTUDIES .... Fred Gray and Rosie Abraham

PETER PAN GOES WRONG opened in New York at the Ethel Barrymore Theatre on Broadway on April 19th, 2023, for a limited season. It was directed by Adam Meggido, the associate director was Fred Gray, the set design was by Simon Scullion, the lighting design was by Matt Haskins, the costume design was by Roberto Surace, the sound design was by Ella Wahlström, the composers were Richard Baker and Rob Falconer, and the choreographers were Dave Hearn and Nancy Zamit. The cast, which included celebrity guest appearances, was as follows:

CHRIS .... Henry Shields
ROBERT .... Henry Lewis
FRANCIS .... Harry Kershaw, Neil Patrick Harris (04/11–05/07), and Ellie Kemper (06/20–06/25)
SANDRA .... Charlie Russell
DENNIS .... Bartley Booz and Jonathan Sayer
ANNIE .... Nancy Zamit
MAX .... Matthew Cavendish
TREVOR .... Chris Leask
JONATHAN .... Greg Tannahill
LUCY .... Ellie Morris
GILL .... Bianca Horn
UNDERSTUDIES .... Ryan Vincent Anderson, Stephen James Anthony, Fred Gray, and Brenann Stacker

CHARACTERS

As with any play-within-a-play, you have the complication of the characters of the actors doing the play-within-the-play and the characters within the play-within-the-play. To try and make it a little simpler the names are laid out in two lists: firstly the actors, the members of the Cornley Drama Society who are putting on the play, and secondly the characters of Peter Pan. *The text always specifies and refers to the actors rather than the characters.*

Members of the Cornley Drama Society

CHRIS is the president of the drama society and plays Mr Darling and Captain Hook.

ROBERT plays Nana the Dog, Peter's Shadow and Starkey.

FRANCIS plays the Narrator and Cecco.

SANDRA plays Wendy Darling.

DENNIS plays John Darling, Mermaid and Mr Smee.

ANNIE plays Mrs Darling, Lisa, Curly and Tinker Bell.

MAX plays Michael Darling, Mermaid and the Crocodile.

TREVOR is the company's stage manager.

JONATHAN plays Peter Pan.

LUCY plays Tootles.

GILL is a Cornley stagehand and later split tracks as a paramedic.

The action takes place on opening night of the Cornley Drama Society's production of Peter Pan, *adapted after J. M. Barrie by Susie H. K. Brideswell.*

Characters in *Peter Pan*

NARRATOR

WENDY DARLING, a girl from London
JOHN DARLING, her younger brother
MICHAEL DARLING, her youngest brother

MARY DARLING, their mother
GEORGE DARLING, their father

NANA THE DOG, the Darling's nursemaid
LISA, the Darling's housekeeper

TOOTLES, one of the Lost Boys
CURLY, another of the Lost Boys

PETER PAN, the boy who would not grow up
TINKER BELL, his fairy
PETER'S SHADOW, his shadow

CAPTAIN HOOK, the captain of the *Jolly Roger*
MR SMEE, his boatswain
STARKEY, his first mate
CECCO, another of his crew

MERMAIDS
THE CROCODILE

SCRIPT NOTES

The stage direction "vamp" denotes improvised dialogue to cover something. In our experience less is always more with this, but also finding believable improvised lines for your versions of the actors is important, and for that reason we haven't included specifics from the original production.

/ denotes the next line beginning over the current line.

AUTHORS' NOTES

Peter Pan Goes Wrong is designed to work on two levels: Firstly, the classic tale of *Peter Pan,* which must be allowed to emerge from the disasters and mishaps within the piece, and secondly, the story of the actors performing the play, which should shine through the cracks in their performances throughout to serve the underlying metanarrative. Everything in the show should be played for truth and not for laughs. When it goes wrong, it hurts!

We've found that, with this piece, it is important to remember that not all of the actors in the play are "bad actors," but simply the victims of circumstance. The comedy comes from their unwavering endeavour to continue and their optimistic belief that their luck can always change.

The same is true of the set, costumes, lighting, sound and other elements of the production. Everything that goes wrong should be a choice, and everything that doesn't go wrong should go right or (in the case of the physical production) look right. The better the production looks, the more of a journey there is to the complete destruction that is caused in the later stages.

Finally, there are moments in the show where Dennis' headset picks up local radio frequencies, resulting in the character parroting advertisment catchphrases and snippets from popular songs. The director/translator or producer is free to alter and update these references and sections based on the location and date of the production. The same is the case for the playbill/programme revealed by Francis during Act One.

PETER PAN GOES WRONG

ACT ONE

The stage is set with a large revolve split into three sections. The first is the nursery. It's displayed to the audience as they walk in and depicts the first scene of the play. The beautifully decorated Darling family nursery has two closed doors; one S. L. *and one* S. R.*, leading to the hall and service quarters of the house. Above the* S. L. *door is a framed painting of the London skyline. A large window is set into the* S. L. *wall. An ornate three-tiered bunk bed stands* S. R.*, complete with a small ladder that allows access to the top bunk. There is a bedside table next to it, and a candle standing on top of it. A wooden train is on the floor in the middle of the room. A large toy chest stands* S. R. *Three sconces protrude from the walls. The only light on the stage is moonlight, which streams in through the window.*

Before the show starts, the theatre lights flicker and fizz occasionally.

The house music fades out, and Trevor steps forward, holding a glass bottle of beer by his side. He silences the audience and reads off of a sheet of paper.

TREVOR. Alright, everybody, welcome to *Peter Pan*. A couple of announcements. The venue kindly requests that patrons ensure they have decanted all drinks into plastic cups.

He realises and hides his beer.

—and also that all members of the audience switch off their cell phones. Do also…

Trevor's cell phone rings. He quickly answers it.

Not now, Tanya, I'm onstage. Yeah, there's quite a few of them… Of course not, it's not *Hamilton*, is it. Yeah, alright, I'll get a photo. Love you, too. Bye.

He hangs up, turns around and takes a selfie of himself in front of the audience. We hear the phone camera noise.

(Continues to read.) Do also remember that photography of any kind is strictly prohibited. One final note, please be aware that the emergency fire exits…are locked. Enjoy the show.

Trevor exits. The house and stage lights come down. Chris and Robert enter from opposite wings. A spotlight comes up on them when they reach the centre.

CHRIS. Good evening and welcome to the Cornley Drama Society's production of J. M. Barrie's classic…

ROBERT. *Peter Pan*!

CHRIS. Please allow me to introduce myself; I am Chris, the director.

ROBERT. And I'm Robert, the codirector.

CHRIS. Assistant director. We're hugely excited to present *Peter Pan*, as this year we've managed to secure a much larger budget than usual, thanks to a sizeable donation from the uncle of one of our cast members, Max. This generous cash injection…

Max enters from the wings and stands, looking at the audience.

Thank you, Max, thank you, Max.

MAX. Thank you.

CHRIS. Thank you, Max.

Max goes.

This generous cash injection has meant that tonight's production will certainly outshine our rather underfunded Christmas show that Robert directed: *Jack and the Bean*.

ROBERT. In one of Chris' productions, due to an ill-timed haircut, Rapunzel had to be imprisoned in a bungalow.

CHRIS. Indeed, that was almost as bad as when Robert insisted on using a real cat in his production of *Puss in Boots,* which became known amongst the company as *Puss Who Was Occasionally in Boots, but Often Refused to Wear His Boots* and then bit a child.

ROBERT. But this year everyone has come together, and we even have my young niece Lucy to play the Lost Boy, Tootles.

CHRIS. Who we are sure will overcome her chronic stage fright this evening. We have taken every possible precaution to ensure the smooth-running of the show.

ROBERT. Including a state-of-the-art radio headset for our actor Dennis to ensure he remembers his lines correctly.

CHRIS. He doesn't know a single line.

ROBERT. But we're feeling optimistic for tonight's family show.

CHRIS. It's not a family show, Robert, it's a proper play. For adults.

ROBERT. Of course it's a family show. Look at how many kids are in. Child. Child. Ugly child. Come on, give us a cheer if you're a child.

Children in the audience cheer, etc.

Great. Now give me a big boo for Captain Hook.

Children boo.

I love Americans, not afraid to be crass.

The company enter with placards and stand in a row behind Chris and Robert.

CHRIS. So, with no further ado, please put your hands together for…

ROBERT. *(Comes in too early.) Peter P…*

CHRIS. J. M. Barrie's…

ROBERT. *(Too early again.) Peter…*

CHRIS. Classic play…

ROBERT and CHRIS. *Peter Pan!*

The cast turn around their placards to reveal the words "ACT ONE OF PETER NAP." They quickly rearrange to spell "ACT ONE OF PETEN PAR." Lights down, all exit. Silence and stillness.

Overture music starts up: loud, dramatic and magical. Sandra (as Wendy) enters, wearing a traditional nightgown, and moves into position C. S. *A pyro-flash suddenly fires* S. R., *and Francis magically appears behind it—as the narrator in a traditional Victorian suit—holding a large, old-fashioned storybook.*

FRANCIS. All children, except one, grow…

Another loud pyro-flash suddenly goes off. Francis screams.

All children, except one, grow up. Wendy discovered that she would grow up when she was very young. She was at a picnic, and her mother said the words, "Oh, I wish you could stay like this forever." And then she knew.

It is this very Wendy, Wendy Moira Angela Darling, along with her two brothers, Michael—

Max enters (as Michael) in a pink babygro.

—and John—

Dennis enters (as John) wearing smart striped pyjamas, glasses and a large radio headset.

—who begin our story.

The spotlight comes up just off C. S., *missing the three actors. The three slowly shuffle into the spotlight. Shortly after, Francis continues their speech and the spotlight slowly moves back to where they were before. The three hurry back into it.*

The setting is their bedroom, on the third floor of a town house in Bloomsbury.

Lights up on the nursery scene.

SANDRA. Come along, boys! Stop playing around, it's time for you to get into your bedclothes.

MAX. It's too early for bed, Wendy. You are turning into Mother.

SANDRA. Well, we are all growing up. We can't be silly children forever.

Sandra reaches up awkwardly to pat Max on the head.

Besides, I should love to be like Mother.

Every time Dennis receives a line feed, we hear a burst of static radio feedback.

DENNIS. *(Holds headset.)* Well, I shouldn't. That would be ever so dreary, Wendy.

MAX. John's right. I can't stand being cooped up in this boring, old nursery. I'm four years old.

DENNIS. *(Holds headset.)* We're young boys, we should be outside climbing trees and playing with toys.

Dennis drops his yo-yo. It isn't attached to the string and rolls along the floor and offstage.

SANDRA. Not every day can be an adventure, John. Now, let's get ready for bed. I can hear Father's footsteps.

Chris enters (as Mr Darling) followed by Annie (as Mrs Darling), both in evening dress. Chris' tie is untied.

CHRIS. Has anyone seen my cuff links?

ANNIE. Oh, George, you are forever losing things.

The lights shift to Francis, followed by the cast in a frozen tableau.

FRANCIS. Their father, George Darling, was a man of business; a little pompous, but with a kind heart.

The cast restart the scene.

CHRIS. I have searched…

Francis continues. The cast suddenly freeze in a tableau again.

FRANCIS. He was far less serene than their mother, Mary Darling, a genteel and elegant woman.

The cast restart the scene.

CHRIS. I have sear…

Francis continues. The cast suddenly freeze in a tableau again.

FRANCIS. Although sometimes he forgot to show it, George loved them all dearly.

Long silence. Lights shift back.

CHRIS. I have searched the house high and low. I put a thing down for a moment and it is as if fairies have danced off with it.

SANDRA. Oh, Father! I would so love to have fairies skipping about the house.

CHRIS. I don't believe in fairies. I believe in cuff links.

DENNIS. *(Holds headset.)* Won't you come and play with us, Father?

Dennis rolls a ball at skittles (bowling pins) set up on the floor but misses. The ball rolls offstage into the wings, and the skittles (cued by a wire) all fall down.

CHRIS. I don't have time for silly games.

MAX. You are so serious, Father.

CHRIS. Grown-ups have to be serious, and little children ought to be. Wendy, have you seen my cuff links?

SANDRA. No, Father.

CHRIS. I mean really, is it me? Or is the world going mad?

Chris hangs his jacket up on a hook on the wall, but the hook is just painted on and the jacket falls to the floor. Chris touches the hook and sees it is painted on.

ANNIE. I'll look in the drawing room, George.

Annie exits through the S. L. door.

DENNIS. *(Holds headset.)* Perhaps Nana has seen them, Father.

CHRIS. That creature is almost certainly the reason they are missing.

Lights shift to Francis.

FRANCIS. It's probably true to say that the Darlings are the only family in Bloomsbury, and probably all of London, to have a dog as a nursemaid. She was a loyal and hardworking Newfoundland named Nana.

The lights shift back, and Robert (as Nana the Dog) is in a dog costume with his face exposed. He enters through a dog flap in the S. R. door.

ROBERT. Woof!

SANDRA, MAX and DENNIS. Nana!

Sandra, Dennis and Max vamp as Robert squeezes through the dog flap with a little difficulty. He trips over the flap as he comes in, and they begin to pat him.

CHRIS. I don't understand all this affection towards that dreadful animal. What about me? Where are my cuff links?

SANDRA. Perhaps Lisa has seen them?

Lights shift to Francis.

FRANCIS. The final member of the household was Lisa, the Darling's housekeeper, different in every way to Mary Darling.

Lights shift back. Annie (as Lisa) enters through the S. L. *door, now dressed completely different.*

ANNIE. I have found your cuff links, Mr Darling. You left them on the dresser!

Lights shift to Francis.

FRANCIS. A sweeter family you've never seen,
with hearts as good as gold,
And on this fateful evening,
our story shall unfold.

Francis, still on their chair, slides sideways offstage. They throw a handful of glitter up as they go. Lights shift back to the scene.

CHRIS. Thank you, Lisa. You have saved my evening. I couldn't have gone to the work party without them.

Annie exits.

(Chuckles.) I suppose I am, Lisa.

Annie reenters quickly.

ANNIE. You are a forgetful man, Mr Darling.

CHRIS. *(Chuckles.)* I suppose I am, Lisa.

Annie exits again, and Chris begins to tie his tie.

Now leave that beast alone, the three of you.

DENNIS. *(Holds headset.)* We're only petting her, Father.

Dennis strokes Robert, and the head comes off Robert's costume.

CHRIS. That dog needs to be taught some discipline. Oh, this tie will not tie! Not around my neck, around the bedpost, oh, yes! Twenty times around the bedpost, but around my neck, no, sir!

MAX. What's wrong, Father?

CHRIS. *(Calls off.)* Mary, this is a nightmare! If I cannot tie my tie, I cannot go out this evening, if I cannot go out this evening, I can never go to the office again, and if I can never go to the office again, I shall lose my job and our children shall be flung out onto the streets!

Annie enters, now dressed as Mrs Darling.

ANNIE. George, really! Allow me to tie it.

Annie begins to tie Chris' tie.

CHRIS. Now, all of you, time for bed and to take your medicine.

MAX. I shan't take my medicine, Father.

DENNIS. *(Holds headset and speaks loudly at Sandra.)* We must take our medicine, Michael.

Annie pulls Chris' tie far too tight. He tries to continue without showing the discomfort.

CHRIS. *(Constricted.)* Thank you, Mother. Perfectly tied.

Chris begins to try to remove his tie.

SANDRA. You must take your medicine.

MAX. But it hurts my throat, Wendy!

CHRIS. *(Constricted and grotesque.)* Hurts your throat, does it?

SANDRA. You must take your medicine, otherwise you shan't grow up to be like Father.

Chris flails around wildly, trying to remove his tie.

MAX. I don't want to be like Father.

CHRIS. *(Even worse. Desperately clutching at his tie.)* Ungrateful child!

Trevor posts a pair of scissors through the S. R. door. Chris grabs them and manages to cut through his tie. He gasps for breath, exhausted.

(Forced calm.) Really, Michael, what an unnecessary fuss you're making.

Chris puts the scissors on the bedside table.

Fetch the medicine bottle, Nana.

Robert bangs his head on the dog flap. The dog flap only opens towards the stage, so Robert stands up and walks offstage through the S. R. door.

When I was a boy, I used to thank my mother and father for giving me my medicine!

Chris trips over the wooden train, and Dennis moves it out of the way, by the S. R. *door.*

I would say, "*Thank you, kind parents! Thank you for giving me bottles to keep me well!*" Ah, here is Nana now.

Robert enters halfway through the dog flap and then gets stuck. He struggles to get free.

Bring me the medicine bottle, Nana…

Robert continues to struggle violently in the dog flap.

Bring me the medicine bottle, Nana… Bring me the medicine bottle, Nana…

Robert puts the medicine bottle in the wooden train and rolls it across the floor to Chris.

Thank you, Nana. Now fetch me a spoon.

Robert tries to squeeze back out through the dog flap but can't. He struggles harder to get free.

DENNIS. *(Holds headset.)* Why don't you take yours first, Father?

CHRIS. Nonsense, John, you shall take yours first, and then I shall take mine.

ANNIE. Boys must take their medicine.

Annie exits through the S. L. *door.*

CHRIS. Quite right. Here is Nana with the spoon now. Bring it to me, there's a good girl.

Robert is still stuck in the door with no spoon; he struggles even harder to get free. The flap hits him on the head.

MAX. Here's the spoon, Father.

Max gives Chris the scissors to use as a spoon.

CHRIS. Thank you, child. Come along, John.

Dennis approaches Chris slowly and unsurely. He shakes his head imploringly as he walks.

Open wide.

Chris pours the medicine through the handle of the scissors, onto the floor.

DENNIS. *(Improvises.)* I don't want it, Father.

CHRIS. *(Improvises.)* None of us wanted this.

Dennis opens his mouth. Chris slowly puts the handles of the scissors inside Dennis' mouth and pulls them out. Radio feedback is heard again.

DENNIS. *(Holds headset.)* Yuck.

Chris pours more medicine into the scissors again.

CHRIS. Now it's your turn, Michael. Medicine for the clever boy who found the spoon.

Chris slowly puts the handles of the scissors into Max's mouth. He tries to pull them out, but they are stuck. He finally yanks the scissors out and accidentally stabs himself in the leg. He screams in pain.

ROBERT. Woof! Woof!

SANDRA. Oh look, Father, Nana is excited! Get down off the bed.

Chris pulls the scissors out of his leg.

CHRIS. Oh, you useless animal! You've gotten dog hairs all over my trousers!

Chris goes over to Robert and rubs his trousers over him.

SANDRA. Silly hound! You've gotten hair all over everyone.

They all rub themselves on Robert.

CHRIS. You daft animal. I always had misgivings about having a dog as a nursemaid.

SANDRA. Father, Nana looks after us so well.

CHRIS. I am sick and tired of everyone coddling that dog! Does anybody coddle me? No, sir! Well, enough is enough. I'm sick of my children being treated like puppies.

Chris slips on the medicine. He quickly stands back up.

It's time for that dog to go out where it belongs, in the yard.

SANDRA, MAX and DENNIS. No!

CHRIS. Lisa!

Annie enters, now dressed as Lisa, through the S. R. door. In doing so, she smashes Robert's face into the toy chest. She is holding a spoon. Annie closes the door.

ANNIE. Yes, Mr Darling?

CHRIS. The spoon! Thank you, Lisa, it's a little late! We used the slotted one! Now, take that wretched animal outside and chain her to her kennel!

ANNIE. Come on, Nana, outside.

Annie opens the door, again smashing Robert's face into the side of the chest. She closes the door to reveal Robert, looking dazed. He continues to try to get loose, and the flap falls down onto his head.

CHRIS. Thank God that animal's gone.

Chris puts his jacket over Robert to hide him.

MAX. Listen to her barking down there.

Robert barks as if from a distance. Radio feedback sound.

ROBERT. *(Faintly.)* Woof, woof.

DENNIS. She is unhappy, Mother.

More feedback sound.

Father.

SANDRA. That is not Nana's unhappy bark; it is how she barks when she senses danger.

CHRIS. Danger? What possible danger could there be in here?

A stage light falls from the rig to the floor with a loud crash as Annie enters, dressed as Mrs Darling, through the S. L. door. Chris, Sandra, Dennis and Max all cower in or around the bed.

ANNIE. What's all this commotion, George?

CHRIS. Mary, my dear. Nothing's wrong, the children were just getting into bed.

ANNIE. Where's Nana?

SANDRA. Lisa locked her outside.

ANNIE. George! But she protects the children.

CHRIS. Protects them from what?

ANNIE. The boy who visits this room.

CHRIS. What nonsense.

Sandra gets out of the bed and Chris follows. Over the following, Sandra moves or dances dramatically around the room.

SANDRA. Mother and I saw him the other evening; he slipped away through the window. Mother ran to slam it shut before he could escape, but he was too nimble; the window shut, and we caught just his shadow, which started dancing across the room.

She ends the speech with a spin, overbalancing a little and hitting the chest.

CHRIS. A dancing shadow? Oh really! What will you come up with next?

ANNIE. I had Lisa lock it in the chest. See for yourself, George. Lisa has the key.

Annie exits through the S. L. door.

SANDRA. I shall get Lisa to fetch the key. Lisa!

Annie opens the S. L. door, now dressed as Lisa.

ANNIE. Yes, Miss Wendy?

SANDRA. Have you the key to the chest?

ANNIE. I shall fetch it at once.

A car horn is heard outside.

Your cab's here, Mr Darling.

CHRIS. Excellent, let's go downstairs…

Another car horn is heard.

ANNIE. Another cab's here, Mr Darling.

CHRIS. Excellent, let's go down…

Another car horn is heard.

ANNIE. A third cab's here, Mr Darling.

CHRIS. Three cabs? *(Looks to Trevor in the wings.)* One for Mary… one for me…and one for…my hat. Let's go downstairs.

ANNIE. I shall fetch the key, Miss Wendy.

SANDRA. Thank you, Lisa.

Annie exits through the S. L. *door.*

CHRIS. Mary, the cab's here!

Annie enters through the S. L. *door, dressed as Mrs Darling.*

ANNIE. The cab's here? I shall fetch my shawl.

Annie exits through the S. L. *door.*

CHRIS. Very good, Mary.

SANDRA. Where is that maid? Lisa!

Annie enters through the S. L. *door, holding the key. She is dressed as Lisa, but the back of her dress is not yet done up, so she crosses sideways, front to the audience.*

ANNIE. I found the key, Miss Wendy.

SANDRA. Now I can show you the shadow, Father!

CHRIS. Oh, Wendy, you really must grow up. There is no shadow.

Annie opens the chest and takes out a cutout of Peter's shadow. Musical spike.

(Not looking.) That will be all, Lisa. I don't have time for this.

SANDRA. Please look, Father!

Annie exits through the S. L. *door.*

CHRIS. I will not indulge these childish games. Mary, the cab's here, we shall be late!

Chris opens the S. L. *door. Annie is midway through getting changed; she covers herself and Chris quickly closes the door. He reopens it, and Annie is changed, now wearing her Mrs Darling costume, but without her shawl.*

ANNIE. The cab's here? Good, I've found my shawl.

The shawl is thrown onto her.

CHRIS. Ah, very good! Come along, Mary!

Sandra has put the shadow back in the chest.

SANDRA. The boy who the shadow belonged to was accompanied by a ball of light, no bigger than my fist, but it darted around the room like a living thing.

CHRIS. I don't believe it for a moment. I'm going downstairs! Someone has to be grown up around here.

Chris opens the S. R. *door but can't fully open it because Robert is still stuck in the flap. He climbs up over Robert and slides through the gap. His foot disappears last, but the door pulls his shoe off. He reaches through and takes it.*

ANNIE. Alright, my dears, time to turn the lights off. Make sure you all…*oh!*

MAX. What is it, Mother?

ANNIE. I thought I saw…a face at the window, nothing there.

Trevor climbs up a ladder into the window frame with a large power saw. He realises and hides from view.

Must be my imagination.

MAX. Mother, I am glad of you.

ANNIE. I am glad of you, too, Michael.

DENNIS. *(Holds headset.)* Won't you sing us a lullaby, Mother?

Radio feedback sound.

(Holds headset.) No, Dennis, speak with feeling, for God's sake. No. No. No. Don't repeat that, you idiot.

ANNIE. Of course, my sweet.

Music starts. Sandra yawns sweetly, followed by Max.

DENNIS. Yawn.

Annie beautifully sings a lullaby to the children as she lights the candle and places it on the end of the bed.

ANNIE. *(Sings.)* Hush now, my Darlings, don't you stir.
Dream of a world of adventure.

As she sings, Annie pulls the drawstring on the sconce by the bed. It goes out. She pulls the drawstring on the next one and it goes out. She goes to the third sconce and pulls the string, it goes out, and the second sconce comes back on. She turns the second sconce off again, and the third one comes back on. She pulls the third drawstring again, it goes out, and the second sconce comes on again. Annie pulls the second sconce off of the wall.

Be at peace, you'll be grown up one day
Till then put your fears away.

Out of sight and out of mind
I tidy the worries I find.

Trevor begins to saw Robert out of the door. Annie sings louder to compete with the sound. Gill comes on with the hammer to help. Francis joins with a large chainsaw. Eventually, Robert is freed and the team exit. Robert exits as well, taking a section of the door with him.

All is quiet and all is calm.
I'll never let you come to harm.

Night-light lit to guide the way,
Until the sun brings in the day,

And as they take their maiden flights,
Guard my sleeping babes tonight.
Guard my sleeping babes tonight.

Annie finishes the lullaby.

MAX. That was beautiful, Mother.

ANNIE. Thank you, my dear.

SANDRA. Can anything harm us when the night-light is lit?

ANNIE. Nothing, precious.

The top bunk of the bunk bed falls sharply onto the middle bunk, trapping Max.

They are the eyes a mother leaves behind her to guard her children.

MAX. *(Muffled under the top bunk.)* Mother, you look pretty tonight.

ANNIE. Are you tucked in, Michael?

MAX. *(Under the top bunk.)* Yes, Mother!

ANNIE. Are you comfortable?

MAX. Yes, Mother.

ANNIE. And you, Wendy?

SANDRA. Yes, Mother.

The middle and top bunk now crash down onto Dennis.

ANNIE. And dear John, are you feeling sleepy?

DENNIS. ARGHHHH!

ANNIE. Good night, my Darlings.

Annie lights a candle on the end of the bed.

Dear night-light that protects my sleeping babes, burn clear and steadfast tonight.

Annie tries to exit through the S. R. door, but it's jammed. She crawls through the sawn-out hole, revealing her underwear.

The lights dim. Tinkling music plays. A light suddenly appears in the window. It darts around the room, searching for something. Trevor wanders onstage and we see he is making the light with a laser pen. He realises his mistake and steps offstage. The light then disappears through the keyhole of the chest. Bells are heard within it. The light reemerges from the chest and disappears through a crack in the S. L. doorway. Silence. Suddenly, Jonathan crashes through the window, breaking it, and is yanked up and down wildly as he flies into the room. He tears the window frame off of its hinges and Trevor runs on to help.*

JONATHAN. Who's flying me?!

Trevor grabs the window frame and exits. Jonathan lands and tries to stand up but is pulled back and knocked into the wall. He stands up again and composes himself.

(Whispering.) Thank heavens I didn't wake the children. Tinker Bell? Tink? Where are you? Have you found my shadow? Do you know where they put it?

Annie enters from D.S., having changed her costume again (now as Tinker Bell). She is covered in fairy lights and bells, and jingles as she walks. As she moves further into the room, we see she has a power cable attached to her back, which leads offstage. She switches on her fairy lights.

There you are! Do you know where they put it?

Annie jingles her bells.

In the toy chest? Where?

* See page 73 for nonflying alternatives.

Annie jingles her bells and walks over to the chest. Her cable is too short and pulls her back, dragging Trevor, who is holding the other end of the power cable, onto the stage. He quickly releases more cable from an extension pack to allow her to move forward and does his best to hide from the audience.

In here?

Annie jingles her bells and points to the chest.

Are you ready, Tink? Don't let it startle you! It's time to get my shadow back, don't let it dance away.

Jonathan goes over to the chest, which bursts open. Robert jumps out, dressed in black Lycra (as the shadow). Music plays. Annie exits, startled, followed by Trevor. Robert dances around the room as the shadow, trying to get away from Jonathan.

Aha! Got you! Now to stick you back where you belong. I shall stick you on with soap!

Jonathan opens a medicine cabinet and takes out a bar of soap. He rubs it on his and Robert's feet. Sandra wakes.

SANDRA. Boy, why are you crying?

Jonathan remembers and starts crying.

JONATHAN. I'm not crying. What's your name?

SANDRA. Wendy Moira Angela Darling. What's yours?

JONATHAN. Peter Pan.

SANDRA. What are you doing?

JONATHAN. I'm trying to stick my shadow back on.

SANDRA. You can't stick a shadow back on with soap. It must be sewn. I shall show you.

Sandra takes a needle from her sewing bag and sews the shadow on in one swift move.

There! It's done! Why don't you try it?

Jonathan springs up and moves around the room. Robert copies his motions.

JONATHAN. Wendy, it's done. Look! Look! Oh, the cleverness of me.

SANDRA. Well, if I did nothing, I shall return to bed.

Sandra sits down sharply on the bed. Dennis and Max groan in pain.

JONATHAN. Wendy, one girl is worth twenty boys.

SANDRA. Do you really think so, Peter?

JONATHAN. Yes, I do!

SANDRA. Well, that's perfectly sweet of you, and I shall get up again.

Sandra stands on the bed, making Dennis and Max groan again.

I'll give you a kiss if you like.

JONATHAN. Thank you. *(Holding out his hand.)*

SANDRA. Don't you know what a kiss is?

JONATHAN. I shall know when you give it to me.

Sandra gives him a large button from her sewing bag.

Now, shall I give you a kiss?

SANDRA. If you please.

They go to kiss. Robert pushes them apart.

ROBERT. Not onstage.

Robert takes an acorn from the brim of Jonathan's hat and gives it to him. Jonathan gives it to Sandra.

Jesus Christ!

SANDRA. An acorn. I shall wear it on a chain around my neck.

Sandra reveals a large acorn already on a chain around her neck.

How old are you?

Jonathan springs across the room. Robert tries to copy Jonathan.

JONATHAN. I don't know, quite young.

A leap move leaves Robert standing in front of Jonathan. Robert says the next line as though he is playing Pan.

ROBERT. I ran away the day I was born!

SANDRA. Ran away, why?

ROBERT. I'll tell you for why!

Jonathan springs across the room again and shoves Robert out of his way to reclaim his role.

JONATHAN. I heard Mother and Father talking of what I was to be when I was a man. I want always to be a little boy and have fun. So I ran away to Kensington Gardens and lived a long time among the fairies.

Jonathan gestures out to the audience, moving his outstretched arm left to right. Robert stands behind Jonathan and copies him. He accidentally slaps the back of Jonathan's head in the process.

SANDRA. You know fairies, Peter?

Jonathan moves towards Sandra.

JONATHAN. Yes, but they're nearly all dead now. You see, when the first baby laughed for the first time, the laugh broke into a thousand tiny pieces and they all went skipping about, and that was the beginning of fairies.

Jonathan places his hand on Sandra's shoulder. Robert removes it.

ROBERT. Easy.

JONATHAN. There ought to be a fairy for every child.

SANDRA. Ought to be? Isn't there?

JONATHAN. Oh no, children know such a lot now, soon they don't believe in fairies, and every time a child says, "I don't believe in fairies," there is a fairy somewhere that falls down dead.

Jonathan flies up to the bed. * *Robert doesn't have a wire, so he has to climb up. He tries to leap off the bedside table, but it breaks underneath him. He clambers up the bed and onto the windowsill. Max and Dennis scream in pain.*

SANDRA. You can fly?

JONATHAN. Of course I can fly!

SANDRA. Where on earth did you learn to do that?

* See page 73 for nonflying alternatives.

JONATHAN. In Neverland.

SANDRA. Oh, Peter, how thrilling.

JONATHAN. Wendy, why don't you come back with me?

*Jonathan springs off the bed and floats gracefully to the floor. As he flies, Jonathan accidentally kicks Robert, who falls backwards out of the window with a huge crash.**

SANDRA. Oh dear, I mustn't! Think of Mother, besides I can't fly!

JONATHAN. I'll teach you.

Robert reenters in pain and stands behind Jonathan again.

SANDRA. How lovely! To fly! But is it far?

JONATHAN. Not far at all, just the other side of the stars.

Jonathan gestures to the window. A cloth of stars pops up outside. Robert copies Jonathan's arm gesture but accidentally leaves his arm over the lit candle. His arm catches on fire, and he panics. Trevor runs onstage with a fire extinguisher, and Gill runs on with a wet cloth. They put him out and then rush back offstage. Robert crawls across the stage and tries to get out through the dog flap but gets stuck halfway.

ROBERT. Not again!

SANDRA. Would you teach John and Michael to fly, too?

JONATHAN. Of course!

SANDRA. John! Michael! Wake up! There is a boy here who is to teach us to fly.

MAX. *(Muffled.)* Fly? I should love to fly.

Sandra and Jonathan lift the bunk off Max and he climbs out of the bed.

SANDRA. He shall take us to Neverland!

DENNIS. *(Extracting himself from the bed.)* Neverland?

Sandra and Jonathan help Dennis out of the bunk bed.

MAX. Can you really fly?

JONATHAN. Look!

MAX. How do you do it?

* See page 73 for nonflying alternatives.

JONATHAN. It's simple, you just need your happiest thoughts and a little bit of fairy dust.

Jonathan blows glitter over the three of them.

SANDRA. Fairy dust! How delightful.

Gill and Trevor enter unmagically and attach Dennis, Max and Sandra to their fly lines. Max elongates his line to buy time for the technical team.

MAX. We're All……Ready to fly.

JONATHAN. Just think of a lovely, wonderful thought, and it will lift you into the air. Michael, what's your happiest thought?

MAX. Fairies, Peter!

JONATHAN. And you, John?

Radio feedback.

DENNIS. Pirates, Peter!

JONATHAN. And you, Wendy?

Trevor roughly checks Sandra's harness.

SANDRA. Mermaids! Oh, Peter, this is such a magical—

Sandra's beautiful speech is interrupted by Trevor.

TREVOR. All clear to fly!

Trevor and Gill exit. Music begins.

MAX. All together?

SANDRA. Yes! One.

ALL. Two. Three.

The fly lines attached to Sandra, Max and Dennis are all suddenly pulled up, but the lines tear off their costumes, leaving them all standing in their underwear in a line onstage. Only the top half of Max's costume has been torn off. He removes the bottom half in order to match the others.

SANDRA. We're flying!

MAX. I feel light as air!

DENNIS. Whee!

JONATHAN. It's time to go. Follow me to the window.

The set begins to revolve to reveal a set of rooftops of London. Music continues. Jonathan lands on the window ledge.

A spotlight comes up on him.

Come on, Tink!

Annie enters and sees everyone in their underwear. She strikes the wardrobe.

Second to the right and then straight on till morning! Here we go!

Jonathan leaps off the window ledge and flies over the rooftops. As the revolve turns, Jonathan is flown straight into the moon, which falls off the set wall, then into a cutout of Big Ben, which breaks. Dennis, Max and Sandra, in their underwear, all scramble to climb through the window. Music swells and the revolve continues to turn.*

(Upside down and in pain.) You see! It's easy when you know how!

MAX. This is tremendous!

SANDRA. I'm flying!

DENNIS. *(Holds headset.)* Woohoo!

JONATHAN. Come on, boys, just believe and you can fly!

Max and Dennis step off the window ledge and fall hard to the floor behind the rooftops. Sandra stands in the window.

SANDRA. Look, Michael and John are doing somersaults!

Max and Dennis do forward rolls on the rooftops in their underwear. The music continues as the set keeps revolving.

JONATHAN. This way! Keep up if you can.

Jonathan flies off upwards into the rig.

SANDRA. Peter, wait for me!

MAX. And me!

DENNIS. *(Holds headset.)* And me!

ALL. Neverland! Here we come!

The set slowly completes its revolve and reveals the forest of Neverland; a beautiful, ethereal forest, covered in glittering

* See page 73 for nonflying alternatives.

flowers. The set consists mainly of two large trees. The tree on S. R. *has a red door on the side of it, with wooden stairs leading up to it. The music stops and Francis slides onstage in their chair, holding the book. They throw glitter.*

FRANCIS. And now we arrive in the forest of Neverland. A world of infinite wonders. Peter and Wendy landed in a forest glade and skipped joyfully through the trees.

So as Peter plays with Wendy
And jealous Tink draws near
Our tale shall continue,
And I shall disappear.

Francis throws a handful of glitter up in the air again. The chair begins to slowly slide sideways. Francis waits, looking out to the audience. The chair stops. Half of their body is still visible. The chair begins to move out again. Their leg gets caught on the tabs and they stop. A hand reaches out from the wing and moves their leg. They move off again. Francis finally disappears. Jonathan, Sandra and Annie enter from behind the trees.

JONATHAN. Wendy, look. We're here!

Annie switches on her fairy lights and we hear an electrical clunk. All the lights immediately go out, plunging the stage into darkness.

Beat.

SANDRA. Oh, Peter, it's beautiful.

JONATHAN. You can see all of Neverland from here, Wendy.

Trevor enters in the darkness and gives a torch to Sandra, which she shines onto her face.

SANDRA. I've never seen trees quite like these before.

Sandra shines the torch onto the stage to highlight the set, but she accidentally shines it on Trevor, who is in a precarious position, trying to pass a torch to Jonathan. They are both startled.

TREVOR and SANDRA. Argh!

SANDRA. Peter, who is that?

JONATHAN. That, Wendy, is Tootles, one of the Lost Boys.

Sandra moves the torch and shines it on Lucy, who looks terrified.

LUCY. *(Totally terrified.)* I'm…Tootles.

JONATHAN. That, Wendy, is Tootles, one of the Lost Boys. The other one was a…err, a mermaid.

The torch shines back onto Trevor who, after a beat, does an impression of a mermaid. Suddenly, the lights snap back on and Trevor leaves, taking the torches.

Hello, Tootles! What news?

Lucy stares in silence at the audience. She tries to run off into the S. L. *trees. One of the trees turns around, revealing itself as Robert in a tree costume (a tube-like structure with a face hole that makes him appear as a regular tree when facing away).**

ROBERT. Lucy. You're doing this.

Lucy tries to speak, but her nerves get the better of her.

LUCY. Pe… Pe…

ROBERT. Peter.

LUCY. I…tell you have something. No! I Peter, tell you something have.

ROBERT. I have to tell you something!

Robert turns away.

JONATHAN. Oh yes? What is it you want to tell me, Tootles?

LUCY. Hooktin Cap…Captain Cook…Hook capped Curly.

Robert turns back.

ROBERT. *(In a boy's voice.)* Captain Hook's kidnapped Curly.

Jonathan and Sandra look at Robert.

SANDRA. Robert, let her do it.

ROBERT. I didn't do anything. I'm just a tree.

Robert starts to slowly back away.

* See page 69 for an alternate scene that does not use a tree costume.

Just an ordinary tree. If I fall in the forest do I make a sound? Who knows?! Who knows?!

Robert backs into another tree on the set and knocks it over. That tree knocks over another, which lands on Lucy with a heavy thump, crushing her leg. We hear a muffled scream from Lucy.

Well, that one made a sound.

Robert exits.

JONATHAN. Captain Hook kidnapped Curly?! Then we must rescue him. Tinker Bell, go and find where they've taken him.

Annie ducks behind a tree. The Tinker Bell light reemerges, and they all watch it fly off. Annie is then seen as she gets up and exits from behind the tree.

Panpipe music suddenly plays. Jonathan quickly gets out his panpipes to mime playing them, but he is too late, and the music stops.

SANDRA. Oh, Peter! You play beautifully…

Suddenly, we hear Chris, Robert and Dennis singing and growling.

JONATHAN. Pirates! Quickly, into the hideout.

Captain Hook's theme music plays, and Jonathan and Sandra go up the stairs on the S. R. *tree and exit. Mist drifts forward.*

Chris (as Hook), Dennis (as Smee), Francis (as Cecco) and Robert (as Starkey with a parrot puppet and peg leg) enter. The music builds to a crescendo as Chris walks through the mist.

CHRIS, DENNIS and FRANCIS. Yarr!!

If the audience boo, Chris tells them, "Shut up."

CHRIS. The glorious sound of a deserted forest, eh lads.

The car horn sound effect plays again.

A cab…

FRANCIS. Not a soul for miles around, Captain Hook.

CHRIS. Aye, Cecco.

Lucy pops up. Chris spots her and pushes her out of sight, telling her, "Get down." Lucy screams in pain; the pirates ad-lib "raws" to cover the screams.

ROBERT. *(Unintelligible through a pirate accent.)* These old, dark woods give me the creeps, Cap'n Hook.

CHRIS. Aye, Starkey. I know what you mean.

Feedback from the headset.

DENNIS. *(Holds headset.)* Captain! We shall find the Lost Boys at…

A moment of radio interference from the headset.

You're listening to WQXR.* That was the Violin Concerto in E minor by Johann Bach.

CHRIS. We shall find the Lost Boys at the Mermaid's Lagoon. You might be right, Smee. Oh, how I'd like to slice their gizzards out.

Headset feedback.

DENNIS. *(Holds headset.)* Just fifteen minutes could save you fifteen percent or more on car insurance.

CHRIS. Thank you, Smee.

Headset feedback.

Dennis starts to sing a popular song from the radio until Chris cuts him off.

Thank you, Mr Smee.

Chris removes Dennis' headset and throws it into the wings.

But most of all I want Peter Pan! For he cut off my arm, Starkey!

ROBERT. *(Unintelligible.)* Disgraceful! That boy has no manners, Captain. Don't you agree, Percy?

Robert squawks an unintelligible reply as Percy the Parrot.

(Unintelligible pirate voice.) Aye, Percy knows how it is.

CHRIS. Exactly. I've waited long to shake his hand with this! Pan flung my arm to a crocodile that happened to be passing by. It was a dark day, hey, Mr Smee.

* Or local classical radio equivalent.

Dennis, without his headset, forgets his line. He shakes his head, lost.

(Prompts.) I've often noticed your fear of that crocodile, Captain Hook.

DENNIS. I've often noticed your fear of that crocodile, Captain Hook.

CHRIS. He got a taste for me flesh that day, Mr Smee.

Dennis forgets his line again.

(Prompts.) He's followed you around ever since, Captain.

DENNIS. *(Comes in with Hook's line.)* That he has, Smee, that he has.

CHRIS. But by lucky chance it swallowed a clock, Captain. So before it can reach you, you hear the clock and bolt.

Dennis takes out his pistol.

DENNIS. What are you doing with your pistol out, Smee?

CHRIS. I wouldn't want to be caught unawares, Captain.

DENNIS. Put that thing away, Smee, or I'll strike you down with my hook.

Dennis grabs Chris' hook. Chris snatches it away.

CHRIS. *No!* Put that thing away, Smee, or *I'll* strike you down with *my* hook! I'm Hook. *You're Smee.*

DENNIS. I'm John.

CHRIS. You're *Smee*! But some day the clock will run down. Ah men, tis the only thing in this world that scares me, but soon I shall have the foolish boy within my grasp!

ROBERT. *(Encouraging the audience.)* Boo.

The audience boo Chris.

CHRIS. Don't boo! Stop booing me. He's right, you are an ugly child. But hold, men! What's this?

Car horn sound effect plays.

A cab. But also there's this. Smoke coming out of this tree stump.

Smoke gently pours from the tree stump.

Tis plain Pan and the Lost Boys live here, among the trees and underneath the ground! Smell, men. Smells like they are cooking goose for dinner.

The smoke blasts Chris, Robert, Francis and Dennis in the face and starts to fill the stage.

Argh! No! No! Go back to the *Jolly Roger.*

Robert, Francis and Dennis rush off, battling through the smoke.

Take Curly to the lagoon, put him out on Marooners' Rock as bait and we'll nab Pan when he tries to save him.

Trevor enters with a large, flattened cardboard box and begins flapping it to clear the smoke. He hits Chris' hook with it by accident and the hook falls off. Trevor runs off. The smoke finally clears.

Avast belay, when I appear
By fear they're overtook,
Naught's left upon your bones when you have shaken claws with Hook!

Chris holds up his hookless hand. He makes a hook shape with his index finger and exits U.S. C. Francis is quickly slid onstage halfway through a costume change, with their trousers around their ankles.

FRANCIS. I'm not ready! And so the dastardly pirates set off with evil intent. Our story now follows Peter and Wendy to the enchanted lagoon. There are many mermaids here and it is the end of a long and playful day.

The stage revolves again to reveal the nursery set. Annie, dressed as Curly, sits on the floor on her phone or iPad, eating a packet of potato chips. The music stops, and the lights come up. She rushes to the wall and tries to blend in with the set.

There are many mermaids here and it is the end of a long and playful day.

The music plays again and the set revolves back the other way to reveal Chris, Robert and Trevor trying to lift the tree off of Lucy. Trevor is frantically using his buzz saw. They realise the audience can see them, so they drop the tree back onto Lucy. They all scream and then recover by making pirate noises, like "argh." The set continues to revolve and reveals the lagoon.

The set has blue fabric cascading down the back to create a waterfall effect. A moon is held up awkwardly from the rooftops. Jonathan and Sandra stand centre by a large rock; Jonathan mimes playing his panpipes. The Neverland music transforms into Jonathan's panpipe-playing. Max, dressed as a mermaid, glides across the stage on Rollerblades. Dennis, also dressed as a mermaid, enters awkwardly on Roller-blades. They skate around and squirt the audience with spray bottles.

There are many mermaids here and it is the end of a long and playful day. The sun's rays have persuaded her to give them another five minutes for one more race over the waters before she gathers them up and lets in the moon.

Dennis skates offstage but is pushed back across the stage by Gill. Dennis screams and crashes into Max, who collides with Francis. They all slide off the stage into the wings together.

SANDRA. Oh, Peter! Mermaids! I would so love to catch one.

Jonathan begins his line, but the panpipe recording hasn't finished.

JONATHAN. Mermaids are fri…

Jonathan resumes playing his panpipes. The recording finishes.

Mermaids are frightfully dangerous creatures, Wendy. Stay close, I'll show you.

Francis enters quickly.

FRANCIS. And with that, Peter and Wendy dived down to the bottom of the twilight lagoon.

Lagoon music begins, and the lights go down. The company enters, dressed in black. They carry UV fish, assorted sea creatures and a model of Peter and Wendy. The fish swim around, colliding with each other as the actors struggle in the darkness. Some of the sea creatures are dropped. When they are picked back up, they end up mismatched (i.e., a mermaid's body with a crab's head and fish that are accidentally assembled into a phallic shape). At the end of the sequence, a large octopus is brought onstage and its fabric tentacles extend around the stage, entangling everyone. There is some bickering through the darkness and suddenly the main lights snap on and the whole cast are seen. Chris motions for the lights to come down and the UV creatures all rush offstage. Everyone exits apart from Max, who is left alone onstage, dancing gleefully with a fish. Chris calls Max from offstage. Gill then rushes across the stage with a large blue sheet to create the sea.

SANDRA. Oh, Peter. I've never seen anything quite like that before.

JONATHAN. Nor have I.

SANDRA. What is this place, Peter?

JONATHAN. This is Marooners' Rock. Tink said the pirates will be bringing Curly here!

ROBERT and DENNIS. *(Singing from off.)* Yarr!

JONATHAN. Here they come! Hide!

Jonathan and Sandra hide out of sight. Dennis (as Smee), still without his headset, Robert (as Starkey) and Annie (as Curly), with her hands tied, enter wearing a cutout of a canoe around their waists. They move with difficulty. Robert rows with large oars and sings with Dennis.

ROBERT and DENNIS. *(Sing.)* Yo-ho! Yo-ho!
A merry hour,
A hempen rope,
And a hey for Davy Jones! Yarr!

DENNIS. Tis good to be upon the water, me lubber. Now we must follow the captain's orders—

Trevor hides behind the blue sheet and holds up a cue card.

(Reads from cue card.) —and hoist Curly onto the rock and leave him there to drown.

ROBERT. *(Unintelligible.)* Out of the boat and up on the rock with you.

Trevor holds up another cue card.

DENNIS. *(Reads from cue card.)* Do as he says. Get out of the boat.

Robert crouches to lower the canoe to the floor. Annie and Dennis step out, treading on the blue sheet, which falls to reveal Trevor retreating to the far corner of the stage. Robert stands back up, accidentally trapping Annie and Dennis' legs inside the side of the boat. He lowers it again to let them out.

ROBERT. Any last words? Speak!

Robert turns and hits Annie with the canoe.

What have you to say, Curly?

ANNIE. These words shan't be my last, as Peter Pan shall save me.

Dennis reads off of another of Trevor's cue cards.

DENNIS. This is a terrible show—

Trevor turns the card around.

—of cowardice Curly. We thought you'd put up more of a fight.

ANNIE. Brave men do not sneak up on defenceless boys, you are the true cowards.

DENNIS. *(Reads from cue card.)* You can't act—

Trevor turns the card.

—in this way when the captain arrives. You have a sharp tongue now, but you shall tremble at the sight of Hook's impressive arse—

Trevor turns the card.

—nal of weapons back aboard the *Jolly Roger.*

Trevor retreats into the wings, embarrassed.

SANDRA. Poor Curly. Help him, Peter.

JONATHAN. Of course, I shall. I'll impersonate Hook. Watch!

A recording of Chris' voice plays as Jonathan mouths the words.

CHRIS' VOICE. Ahoy there, you lubbers!

DENNIS. *(Reads from cue card from the wings.)* Tis the captain. He must be swimming out to us! *(Calls out.)* Just bringing Curly up onto the rock, Cap'n.

CHRIS' VOICE. Set him free.

DENNIS. *(Reads from cue card.)* Cut him free?

CHRIS' VOICE. My orders? Nonsense! Release him, you blithering imbeciles! Cut him free!

ROBERT. *(Unintelligible.)* Aye, Cap'n!

Robert goes to untie Annie's hands but knocks her over by accident. He turns back and knocks Dennis over.

Aye aye, Cap'n! I'll cut him free!

*Robert struggles to get out of the canoe and finds himself stuck. He drops his sword and can't reach it. He tries to tell Dennis to release Annie himself, but his words are unintelligible—"Why don't you cut him free, Smee?," "Pass me the sword" and "I can't set him free, I'm stuck in the boat." Dennis doesn't understand and responds in a similarly garbled pirate voice: "I don't understand what you're saying," "I don't remember rehearsing this section," etc. Robert attempts to clarify, still unintelligibly: "We haven't rehearsed this section—this is a new emergency section where you give me the sword!" Their exchange escalates into an unintelligible pirate argument. Misunderstanding, Dennis hands Robert the "deep blue sea" prop, then the oar. Defeated, Robert turns back to Annie, who has retrieved the dropped sword. Robert takes the sword from Annie, who shows her hands are not tied.**

(Just decipherable.) He's free, Cap'n!

Dennis retreats to the rocks, and Gill and Trevor recreate the sea from the top of the scene. They hold either end of the blue sheet. Annie dives underwater.

CHRIS. *(Calls from off.)* I'm swimming out to you, boys!

Chris (as Hook) and Francis (as Cecco) enter, pretending to swim.

Now, where is the Lost Boy?

Annie pops up and is clearly seen by Chris.

No.

Annie exits.

Now, where is the Lost Boy?

* The section in which Robert and Dennis argue unintelligible can be improvised and different each night. The stage directions give an example of what that conversation could be.

DENNIS. *(Reads from cue card.)* That's alright, Captain, we followed your orders and let him go.

CHRIS. You blundering blockheads, I said no such thing.

FRANCIS. If you didn't give the orders, Captain, who did?

CHRIS. Perhaps it be the dark spirits that haunt this here lagoon, Cecco.

ROBERT. Spirits, Cap'n?

Eerie lagoon music starts.

CHRIS. Spirit! Dost hear me?

CHRIS' VOICE. I hear you!

ROBERT'S VOICE. Cut there. Passable. Acceptable. Now get out, I want to record my audition tapes.

CHRIS' VOICE. Oh, for God's sake—

The recording cuts out.

CHRIS. Who are you, stranger? Speak!

CHRIS' VOICE. I am James Hook! Captain of the *Jolly Roger*!

CHRIS. It can't be!

ROBERT. *(Unintelligible. Puts his hand to his ear.)* But what's that sound, Cap'n?

CHRIS. It is a ticking clock! Tis the crocodile!

Max (as the crocodile), lying on top of a wheeled trolley, rolls onstage. The ticking sound continues.

FRANCIS. Captain, the crocodile's come to finish you off!

CHRIS. Spirit, if you are Hook, then who am I?

CHRIS' VOICE. A cod fish!

The cast freeze as the audio skips into…

ROBERT'S VOICE. Cut. Yes, I suppose that'll do. Excellent! We have all the recordings now.

CHRIS' VOICE. Robert, there's something I wanted to talk to you about.

ROBERT'S VOICE. What is it?

CHRIS' VOICE. I'm concerned about Jonathan and Sandra.

ROBERT'S VOICE. Oh, absolutely, their behavior is just lewd!

CHRIS' VOICE. Exactly. Jonathan's playing Peter Pan and Sandra's playing Wendy; they shouldn't be sleeping together.

ROBERT'S VOICE. He's supposed to be the boy who wouldn't grow up, not the boy who couldn't keep it in his pants.

Jonathan and Sandra edge away from each other.

And she's just as bad! Flirting with everybody! It's no wonder Max is obsessed with her.

CHRIS' VOICE. Oh, well that must be why he keeps asking if he can play Peter Pan, he just wants to get closer to her.

ROBERT'S VOICE. He didn't? He wants to play Peter?!

CHRIS' VOICE. He's learnt all the lines!

ROBERT'S VOICE. But Max can't act! He cannot act to save his life. He's terrible as Michael and the crocodile. He's playing it like a mammal.

CHRIS' VOICE. I know he's bad, but we need his uncle's money. He's invested eighty thousand dollars in this production, Robert! It's the only reason he's here.

ROBERT'S VOICE. What a loser.

CHRIS' VOICE. Oop, left the microphone on—

The recording ends. Silence. They all glare at each other. Then they all finally look to Max. Max looks to Sandra. Jonathan puts his arms around her. Sandra looks away from Max. Max slowly exits S. R. *The cast turn to Chris. Pause. If the audience boo, Chris tells them, "Grow up."*

CHRIS. Tis Peter Pan!

Jonathan leaps out from behind the rocks. The rest of the cast scatter to make space for the fight.

JONATHAN. Tis I!

CHRIS. Take him dead or alive!

SANDRA. Do be careful, Peter!

CHRIS. Come and face me, Pan!

Dramatic music starts to build.

JONATHAN. I shall, old and weary Hook!

CHRIS. You are no match for my might, blade and hook, Pan!

JONATHAN. En garde, Captain Hook!

The fight begins, swift and slick. Jonathan starts flying higher and higher around Chris, and the waterfall fabric on the set is accidentally torn down.[*]

CHRIS. Foolish Pan!

JONATHAN. Take that, you fiend!

CHRIS. Vainglorious boy! I shall split your bones with my hook!

JONATHAN. Nothing ever hurts me! I'm Peter Pa—

Jonathan suddenly starts to shake wildly on his fly line, jerking up and down. Chris loses his hook in the fight. He goes to get it but trips and gets tangled in the blue sea sheet. Robert turns and hits Trevor (who is still holding the other end of the blue sheet). Robert turns back and hits Dennis, who falls into Sandra.

I'm Peter… Pa… I'm Peter… Pa… Pet… Pa… Nothing ever hurts me! I'm Peter Paaan!

Jonathan shoots up out of sight into the rig, screaming. The cast look up to the rig helplessly, waving for Jonathan to be brought down.

CHRIS. You'll die by my blade, Pan!

JONATHAN. To die will be an awfully big adventuuuuure!

We see Jonathan's body suddenly drop from the rig and straight down onto the stage.

A large banner falls down into view, reading "JACK AND THE BEAN" with a picture of Robert smiling, dressed as "Jack," shrugging and holding one single bean. Music cuts out. Silence.

CHRIS. Intermission!

Blackout. Tabs. House lights and music.

End of Act One

* See page 74 for nonflying alternatives.

ACT TWO

Robert enters through the house tabs and addresses the audience.

ROBERT. Welcome back everyone, Chris has asked me to come out and stall for a few moments—

CHRIS. *(Off.)* Speak!

ROBERT. Speak for a few moments as the codirector—

CHRIS. *(Off.)* Assistant director!

ROBERT. Thank you. Chris is just finishing up dealing with the paramedics. But I am delighted to report that little Lucy is perfectly…alive.

Now, I do apologise for the technical issues we've been experiencing, apparently we are running too many electrical appliances through the theatre, including the revolving stage, all the lighting and sound equipment, and of course, my Ford Mustang electric car. However, we are confident we have resolved the issue—

ROBERT'S VOICE. Robert Grove audition tape twelve. New York.

ROBERT. Sorry about that—

ROBERT'S VOICE. I've got buffalo wings in my glove compartment!

ROBERT. …One of my audition tapes there… Now before we stopped, the more keen-eyed of you will have seen that Peter Pan took a rather nasty, unrehearsed fall. Obviously he wasn't thinking his happy thoughts. Nor will he be when he regains consciousness. However, do not fear, we are able to continue, and I'm sure you will barely notice the difference.

Besides, his injuries are certainly less severe than those sustained in the first act of our previous production of *Oliver! The Musical.* When, during the number "Food, Glorious Food," our portly Mr Bumble tripped back onto one of the frailer workhouse children, crushing him. Regrettably, I had parked in the ambulance bay, and the paramedics were unable to get to the boy in time, and he sadly passed. I cannot help but feel partially responsible for that tragic event, as it was my vehicle that stopped medical professionals getting to him, and also because I was playing Mr Bumble.

Silence.

Anyway, as they say in Hollywood: "on with the show business."

The cast once again enter with placards and stand in their line.

Please put your hands together for…

The cast turn around their placards to reveal the words "A TON OF WET PET CRAP."

Act Two of *Peter Pan*!

They all exit into the wings. The lights come up on the forest scene; a picnic table is placed on the centre of the revolve. Sandra (as Wendy) lays dishes of imaginary food on top of it.

Francis, seated on their chair, gracefully slides into position but faces the wrong way. They throw glitter, realise they are facing U.S.*, turn around and begin the narration.*

FRANCIS. We have now reached the evening which was to be known among them as the night of nights, because of its adventures and their upshot.

The day, as if quietly gathering its forces, had been almost uneventful and now the children were just about to return to Wendy for their evening meal.

The meal happened to be an imaginary one,

With nothing whatever on the table;

Not a mug, nor a crust, nor knives.

However, Wendy called the Lost Boys to dinner,

As if for the greatest feast of their lives.

Francis slowly squeezes through the backwards chair, so they are still facing the right way, throws glitter and is pulled off.

SANDRA. Come along, boys! Michael!

Max appears from behind a tree.

MAX. Yes, Wendy!

SANDRA. John!

Dennis appears, now wearing his headset again.

DENNIS. *(Holds headset.)* Yes, Wendy!

SANDRA. Tootles!

Annie (as Tinker Bell) enters S. R. *A beat later, Lucy (as Tootles) enters* S. L.*, now on crutches, and is pursued by Robert (as the tree). Lucy is even more terrified than before.*

ROBERT. Get onstage, Lucy!

SANDRA. It's time for dinner!

Headset feedback.

DENNIS. *(Holds headset.)* Oh, I do love Neverland!

Headset interference sound effect.

And now for the weather report.

MAX. I hear this evening's meal is imaginary.

SANDRA. So it can be anything you want it to be.

ALL. Anything?

SANDRA. Anything!

The below song is an upbeat musical theatre number with a Disney feel.

(Sings.) You can have steak or salami,
You can have chestnuts or cheese,
The only thing to remember
Is the magic word…

ALL. *(Sings.)* What?

SANDRA. *(Sings.)* Please!

MAX. *(Spoken.)* So I can have anything I can think of?

SANDRA. *(Spoken.)* Of course!

MAX. *(Sings.)* I could have lobster or lettuce.

SANDRA. *(Sings.)* You could have pastry or pies.

MAX. *(Sings.)* I could have dumplings or damsons.

DENNIS. *(Holds headset, sings.)* Your Uber has arrived!

Dance begins for the chorus.

SANDRA. *(Sings.)* With give and take then you can make,
Whatever you can conceive,
With faith and trust and fairy dust,
And the world of make believe.

As the chorus begins, Gill and Annie join in the dance.

ALL. *(Sings.)* With give and take then we can make,
Whatever we can conceive,
With faith and trust and fairy dust,
And the world of make believe.

MAX. *(Spoken.)* But Wendy, where's Peter?

SANDRA. *(Spoken.)* This is Neverland, Michael; he could be anywhere you want him to be! *(Sings.)* He could be fighting off pirates.

MAX. *(Sings.)* Or chasing a horse!

SANDRA. *(Sings.)* He could be riding a star.

Francis is slid on in the chair.

FRANCIS. *(Sings.)* Impossible!

SANDRA. *(Sings.)* Of course!

Francis is slid off.

MAX. *(Sings.)* I could be a steam-engine driver.

ANNIE. *(Sings.)* Or a carnival clown.

SANDRA. *(Sings.)* You could be a prince fighting dragons.

DENNIS. *(Holds headset, sings.)* The A train is down!*

MAX. *(Sings.)* I'll be a warrior winning the war!

SANDRA. *(Sings.)* I'll be a lawyer learning the law!

ANNIE. *(Sings.)* I'll be a pastor protecting the poor!

All climb up onto chairs.

Dennis loudly sings a line from another musical that he picks up on his headphones.

The music shifts to a tap dance break. Lucy struggles to tap with her broken foot.

ALL. *(Sings.)* With give and take then we can make,
Whatever we can conceive,

* Another local reference can be used here.

With faith and trust and fairy dust,
With sticks and stones and bags of bones,
With ups and downs and all arounds,
With hops and skips and broken bits,

A brief break where Robert appears as the shadow and reprises his dance. He accidentally breaks through one of the steps on the S. R. stairs and gets stuck. The main song snaps back in.

SANDRA. With courage!

DENNIS. Honor!

MAX. Valor!

ANNIE. Speed!

SANDRA. Heroes!

MAX. Villains!

SANDRA. Goblins!

ANNIE. Greed!

SANDRA. Princes!

ANNIE. Wizards!

SANDRA. Sandstorms!

MAX. Blizzards!

DENNIS. Action!

ANNIE. Fighting!

MAX. Thunder!

DENNIS. Lightning!

ALL. *(Sings.)* Whatever you can conceive!
And the world of make believe!
And the world of make be—
LIEEEEEVE!!

Robert is handed a plate to join in the final tableau. As he quickly raises his plate, he accidentally hits Lucy in the face. She falls through the door and out of sight. The song finishes.

Annie, Robert and Gill skip off.

MAX. I do so love it here.

SANDRA. How wonderful!

MAX. I wish we could stay here forever.

SANDRA. Michael, you must not forget we have a mother and father waiting for us back at home. Oh, I can hear Peter outside. Quickly, all of you, you know how he likes you to meet him at the door.

We hear the flying mechanism squeaking. Trevor (as Peter Pan) is slowly winched in. He clutches a script and wears Peter Pan's hat. He looks terrified.*

TREVOR. *(Reads stage direction from the script.)* Peter enters.

SANDRA. Peter, you're back.

MAX. Any adventures, Peter?

TREVOR. I battled with two tigers and a dozen pirates.

SANDRA. How exciting.

TREVOR. I love adventures, Wendy! *(Reads stage direction.)* Peter flies around the room, showboating and full of mirth.

Trevor is jerked erratically back and forth around the stage, smashing into the set.

SANDRA. Oh, Peter! No one flies better than you!

TREVOR. I shall tell you my tale. *(Reads stage direction.)* Peter lands nimbly.

Trevor plummets down heavily onto the floor.

SANDRA. This sounds wonderful, but first you must have your dinner.

Max gives Trevor a plate. He sits down at the table and begins to eat.

TREVOR. Peter begins to eat Tinker Bell.

Trevor misreads where the full stop is in the sentence.

Has behaved most oddly since her return.

SANDRA. Perhaps she is angry with me?

TREVOR. Fairies have to be one thing or the other because being so small they have room for only one feeling at a time.

Trevor slowly begins to fly up from his seat; he tries to resist and carry on eating. Max and Dennis try to hold him down.

* See page 74 for nonflying alternatives.

Throughout the dialogue, he continues to rise until he ends up hanging upside down, facing away from the audience with his backside hanging out of his flying harness.

SANDRA. I fear Tinker Bell is jealous of me.

TREVOR. Why should she be jealous? Girls are so puzzling. *(Reads stage direction.)* Looks at Wendy seriously for a moment.

Trevor pushes himself off the set and swings towards Sandra before swinging back into the set with a thump.

SANDRA. The three of us do worry about you, Peter.

TREVOR. But Wendy, there is nothing to worry about!

Trevor tries to turn himself the right way up but spins all the way around in his harness.

No one knows Neverland better than I, and I cannot help being at the centre of adventures.

SANDRA. But it sounds awfully dangerous, Peter. You are careful out there, aren't you?

Trevor drops down to the floor heavily, then is pulled back up violently to his feet by the fly line.

TREVOR. Don't worry, Wendy, nothing ever hurts me; I'm Peter Pan.

SANDRA. Peter, I do fear for you though, the world can be such a frightening place. What if Captain Hook were to capture you? I couldn't bear to see you die.

TREVOR. Don't worry, Wendy. *(Reads stage direction.)* Peter flies up onto the table.

Trevor starts to ascend.

(Shouts into the wings.) No he doesn't, he doesn't—

Trevor lands gently.

He's fine. Don't worry, Wendy. To die would be an awfully big adventure—

As he steps onto the table, a loose plank of wood shoots up and hits him in the face, knocking him unconscious. The Peter Pan hat lands on the table. Trevor remains suspended in the air. From offstage, Robert pokes him with the end of a broom in an attempt to wake him. Robert then enters, checks Trevor's *pulse, and, satisfied that he's still alive, pushes Trevor's motionless body offstage. Robert remains onstage, looking at Peter Pan's hat as remaining cast members exchange uncertain looks, trying to figure out what to do. Eventually, Robert picks up the hat and softly sings something like "Food, Glorious Food" to himself.* He tosses the hat back onto the table, backs away and exits. Dennis reaches for the hat but is interrupted by the sound of radio feedback.*

DENNIS. *(Holds headset.)* Not you, Dennis, walk away.

Dennis exits with his hands in the air. Max looks at the audience. (Hopefully they will encourage him to take the hat.) Max then takes the hat. Throughout the rest of the scene, he plays the role of Peter Pan well.

MAX. When you die, you fly off over the waters and the stars guide your way.

SANDRA. Peter… The stars do look beautiful in Neverland.

MAX. Stars are beautiful, Wendy, but they may not take an active part in anything, they must just look on forever. It is a punishment put on them for something they did so long ago that no star now knows what it was. So the older ones have become glassy-eyed and seldom speak by their winking, but the little ones still wonder.

SANDRA. Oh, Peter.

Max picks up the panpipes from the floor.

MAX. I do so love adventures.

Max goes to play the panpipes, but the wrong sound cue is played. They listen again in horror.

CHRIS' VOICE. Sound cue recording twenty-one. Panpipes. Take one.

The sound of air being blown through the panpipes is heard.

Where's that handbook? Mother, did you move my panpipes handbook?

The sound of the door being opened is heard.

Oh, Max, what are you doing here?

* See note on songs/recordings at the back of this volume.

MAX'S VOICE. Hi. Sorry, I just wanted to ask about Peter Pan again.

CHRIS' VOICE. Max, we have been over this, you're playing Michael Darling and the crocodile.

MAX'S VOICE. But no one likes the crocodile. Everyone likes Peter and...Peter gets to do all the fun stuff.

CHRIS' VOICE. You mean like kissing Sandra?

MAX'S VOICE. Maybe...

CHRIS' VOICE. You know she's in a relationship with Jonathan?

MAX'S VOICE. Yes! Because he is playing Peter.

CHRIS' VOICE. I hardly think that's—

MAX'S VOICE. I'm in love with Sandra.

Beat.

CHRIS' VOICE. Well, that's neither here nor there and certainly no reason to recast...

MAX'S VOICE. I keep dreaming about her though, Chris.

CHRIS' VOICE. Alright, thank you, Max. Now, if you don't mind...

MAX'S VOICE. She's my soulmate.

CHRIS' VOICE. Max. If you don't mind, I need to finish recording the panpipes.

MAX'S VOICE. Oh, OK. Er... Sorry.

The sound of Max leaving and closing the door is heard.

CHRIS' VOICE. Note: Don't use take one.

The recording ends. The whole cast stare at Max. A long silence. Max plays a few notes on the panpipes.

MAX. I... I...

Francis is suddenly fired onto the stage at an alarming speed, causing them to fall off their chair. They hurriedly stand up and throw glitter. The rest of the cast freeze.

FRANCIS. But little did Peter, Wendy or the Lost Boys know that up upon the ground above their home, Hook, leading his crew, lurked among the trees, waiting for them to come out into the night.

Chris (as Hook) peers menacingly around a tree. If the audience boo him, he shouts, "Oh, grow up!" at them.

Down in Peter's hideout,
Wendy began to understand,
It was time for her, John and Michael
To fly home from Neverland.

The chair is whisked offstage just as Francis goes to sit down, causing them to fall. They recover, but the chair is then pushed back on from the wings, slamming into Francis. The chair exits with Francis slumped on top of it.

SANDRA. Peter, if you would come back with me, I'm sure my mother and father would adopt you.

MAX. No, Wendy, I flew back once to see my mother, but the window was barred, and she had forgotten about me and there was another little boy asleep in my bed.

SANDRA. Are you sure all mothers are like that?

MAX. Yes.

SANDRA. Peter, what are your exact feelings for me?

MAX. My fe…

The soundboard malfunctions, and we hear a burst of different recordings and sound cues from earlier in the show mixed together.

CHRIS' VOICE. Sound recording twenty… .

ROBERT'S VOICE. Max can't act.

MAX'S VOICE. …I'm in love with Sandra…

CHRIS' VOICE. …neither here nor ther…

MAX'S VOICE. I keep dreaming about her…dreaming about her…dreaming about her…dreami… She's my soulmate…soulmate…in love with Sandra… In love…dreaming about her…soulmate…oulmate…oulmate…

ROBERT'S VOICE. I've got buffalo wings in my glove compartment!

The recording cuts out. Max stands in silence, looking at Sandra.

MAX. My feelings are those of a devoted son, Wendy.

SANDRA. I thought so. And in that case, I must leave at once. Oh, Peter, say you'll come with us.

MAX. No. I shall stay here and always be a little boy and have fun.

SANDRA. Then you must…kiss me goodbye, Peter.

Max reaches into the brim of his hat and produces the thimble.

Oh, Peter. I meant a real kiss.

MAX. A real kiss?

SANDRA. You do not know what a real kiss is?

MAX. No. I do not.

SANDRA. Then I will show you.

Jonathan appears at the side of the stage, wearing a bandage on his head. Sandra runs past Max to Jonathan and kisses him. Max stands there.

JONATHAN. This is a real kiss?

SANDRA. Yes, Peter, a real kiss.

Dennis reenters, pushing Lucy in a wheelchair.

JONATHAN. It's time for you to go now, no fuss, no blubbering. I hope your mother is happy to see you again. Be careful you don't run into pirates. Or that crocodile *(To Max.)* that nobody likes.

Jonathan takes back his hat and the acorn. Max joins the others.

SANDRA. Peter, you will remember to take your medicine, won't you?

JONATHAN. I won't forget.

SANDRA. Goodbye, Peter.

JONATHAN. Goodbye, Wendy. Goodbye, boys.

ALL. Goodbye.

Chris (as Hook) and Robert (as pirate Starkey) appear in the doorway. Francis bounds on without their chair and throws glitter.

FRANCIS. The travellers start upon their journey—

Francis' chair rolls on.

I don't need you anymore!

The chair is sheepishly removed. If the audience "awww" the chair, Francis says, "It's a chair!" Hook's theme music begins.

Little witting that Hook had issued his silent orders: his men to hide in wait among the trees. As the children walk by, they are plucked, trussed and gagged.

As the narration continues, the cast silently enact the kidnapping. Sandra and Dennis are taken first. Robert, Chris, and Max then attempt to exit through the red door in the tree but find that the wheelchair won't fit. Robert roughly lifts Lucy out of her chair, hammering her injured foot with his hand as he forces her through the door. Chris gets his hook caught on the wheelchair, and as Robert removes the chair, he slams the door on Chris's arm. Chris then descends the stairs unsteadily.

Hook signed to his dogs to be gone, and they departed through the forest. The screams and cries lost to Peter as he had fallen asleep in his chair, dreaming of a boy who is never here, nor anywhere, the only boy who could beat him. Once the pirates had carried the children a few more paces into the night, Hook crept into the clearing…

And with stealth, cunning, guile and craft, he added poison to the medicine draught.

Francis exits. Chris creeps to the front of the stage, standing in front of Jonathan.

CHRIS. Now, where is Peter Pan? Where is Peter Pan?

Chris interacts with audience if they boo/shout, etc. If they tell him where Pan is, he responds, "I know he is. I directed the play. I told him to go there."

Oh, there he is.

Chris picks up a small bottle.

Medicine… Poison…

Chris struggles to lift the lid off the bottle of poison with his hook. He vamps with the audience: "Stay out of it," "You are not making this any easier!," "Stop laughing, this is a serious play. Why can't you be like that woman. Two hours she hasn't laughed once," etc. Eventually, he manages to lift the lid off and goes to pour his vial of poison into the medicine bottle, but he realises the medicine bottle has a screw top and is impossible to open with the hook. He is forced to ask an audience member to open it for him. Chris vamps with the audience again: "It's easy if you use two hands," "Thank you very much for helping me kill Peter Pan," etc. He adds the poison into the medicine bottle and leaves it on the table in front of Jonathan as he exits. Annie (as Tinker Bell) enters from S. R.*, lit up on her cable. Jonathan wakes up.*

JONATHAN. Wendy? Tink! Tinker Bell! What's the matter?

Annie jingles her bells.

What's that? Wendy and the boys captured by pirates? I'll rescue her! Where's my dagger?

Annie jingles her bells. She jumps in the air, and Trevor (now bandaged) is again pulled onstage by the power cable. He unspools more cable for Annie.

That? It's just my medicine.

Annie jingles her bells.

Poisoned? Who could have poisoned it?

Annie points to the audience member who helped Hook open the medicine bottle.

I promised I would take it, and I will.

Annie jingles her bells fiercely and tries to take the medicine bottle. Jonathan struggles to get it back.

Tink! No! What are you doing? That's my medicine! Stop drinking it! Stop it! Stop it!

Annie finally takes the bottle and unscrews the lid, but trips on the cable around her leg, spilling the poison over herself and the power pack of the extension lead. An electrical fizz is heard, and Annie's fairy lights suddenly glow intensely bright. A sudden pop follows, plunging the stage into darkness. Sparks fly. Silence. Whispering is heard, then the sound of the power rebooting as the lights come back on. Annie lies on the floor, unconscious, her fairy lights out. Jonathan cautiously approaches her. Trevor steps into view, watching her.

Tink…? You drank it… It was poisoned and you drank it to save my life… Tink…? Tink are…are you alright? Tink?

Jonathan looks into the wings, scared, and signals for help.

Chris…

Chris enters and goes over to help. Francis, Robert and Gill enter. Vamp. The mood becomes quite serious. Out of the murmuring, we hear Robert saying the word "electrocuted" a little too loudly.

CHRIS. Who's the first-aider?

ROBERT. Who's the first-aider?

TREVOR. *(Gestures to Annie.)* She's the first-aider.

Sandra enters from the red door in the S. R. tree.

SANDRA. Robert, did you crush her? Call an ambulance…and move your car.

Lucy enters in her wheelchair with Max chasing behind.

CHRIS. Do something to cover.

Francis tries their best to improvise some "filler" but fails. The cast stare mournfully at Francis. Lucy tries to speak up.

LUCY. *(Very nervous still.)* …We…have to believe in fairies.

ROBERT. Not now, Lucy, this is serious!

LUCY. I believe…in fairies.

ROBERT. That's enough! Thank you.

Lucy stands up with difficulty and begins to clap.

LUCY. …I believe in fairies.

ROBERT. Grow up, Lucy!

Max joins in.

LUCY and MAX. I believe in fairies.

Dennis, Francis, Trevor and Sandra join in as well, one by one. Gradually, the cast and audience begin clapping and chanting, "I believe in fairies." Eventually, even Chris and Robert join in, but Jonathan does not. As the shouting reaches a peak, Annie suddenly springs up and coughs out a puff of smoke. The cast freeze, shocked.

CHRIS. Places!

All but Annie and Jonathan exit.

JONATHAN. Well done! Well done! Thank you! You've saved Tinker Bell! And now to rescue Wendy! Come on, Tink! To the pirate ship! It's Hook or me this time!

Music begins to play on the speakers. The set begins to slowly revolve to reveal the lagoon set, now containing the deck of the Jolly Roger. *Chris (as Hook), Francis (as Cecco), Robert (as Starkey), Sandra (as Wendy), Max (as Michael) and Dennis (as John) are on the deck and sing.*

ALL. Yo-ho! Yo-ho!
Yo-ho, the pirate life,
The flag of skull and bones,
A merry hour, a hempen rope
And hey for Davy Jones!

Avast, belay, yo-ho, heave to,
A-pirating we go,
And if we're parted by a shot,
We're sure to meet below.

Yo-ho, the pirate life,
The flag of skull and bones,
A merry hour, a hempen rope,
And hey for Davy Jones!

A-sailing on the seven seas,
What better life is there?
And any honest Jack or John
Had better best beware!
Had better best beware!

Yo-ho, the pirate life,
The flag of skull and bones,
A merry hour, a hempen rope,
And hey for Davy Jones!

There's not a sea we never sailed,
Or drink we never drank,
And any lubber says not so,
We'll see him walk the plank!
The last naysayer took a swim,
and then the lubber sank.

Yo-ho! Yo-ho!

Yo-ho, the pirate life,
The flag of skull and bones,
A merry hour, a hempen rope,
And hey for Davy Jones!

Come raise the mast and swab the deck,
And let the anchor sink,
We'll stab and kill and plunder too,
And then we'll have a drink.

Yo-ho, the pirate life,
The flag of skull and bones,
A merry hour, a hempen rope,
And hey for Davy Jones!

We have no wives; we have no woes,
Well never show no fear,
You do what you must do to live,
When you're a buccaneer!
When you're a buccaneer!

Yo-ho, the pirate life,
The flag of skull and bones,
A merry hour, a hempen rope,
And hey for Davy Jones!

Ye scurvy dog, give me your gold,
And hoist! We'll hoist the sail,
Remember if you try to squeal,
A dead man tells no tales!
We'll never take no quarters mate,
We won't end up in jail.

Yo-ho! Yo-ho!

Yo-ho, the pirate life,
The flag of skull and bones,
A merry hour, a hempen rope
And hey for Davy Jones!
And hey for Davy Jones!

Yaar!

The revolve keeps turning and the following happens throughout the song:

PIRATE SHIP ONE: *As the ship arrives* C. S., *Dennis throws an anchor off the deck. But the revolve doesn't stop, and the* Jolly Roger *revolves back out of sight. Dennis slowly reels the anchor back in.*

NURSERY ONE: *Lucy, her leg still bandaged, is in the wheelchair. Trevor makes her sign documents titled "LEGAL DISCLAIMER" while a paramedic treats her. They slowly realise they are now in view and look out at the audience. They all start to do the pirate's dance, and the paramedic joins in last.*

FOREST ONE: *Jonathan is talking to Annie (still as Tinker Bell) and trying to comfort her. They start to kiss.*

PIRATE SHIP TWO: *The pirate ship comes around again. The scene is exactly the same as it was before, and the group is confident that the revolve will stop this time. It doesn't stop. Dennis throws the anchor but forgets to hold the other end of the rope. The whole thing flies off the revolve and into the wings.*

NURSERY TWO: *The pirate ship continues back around, and the nursery set is revealed again. Gill/Paramedic continues to treat Lucy. Trevor has opened a fuse box in the floor, with wires coming out, and is desperately trying to fix the issue. Robert enters from the pirate ship, roughly lifts Lucy out of her chair, and takes her back to the* Jolly Roger. *As he turns, Lucy's feet hit Trevor in the face. Left alone, Trevor and Gill/Paramedic return to joining the pirate dance to save face.*

FOREST TWO: *Annie and Jonathan are now lying on the table, kissing passionately. Sandra stands at the red door, watching in horror. She runs at Jonathan and slaps him, jumps on his back and hits him with his hat. Annie rushes offstage.*

PIRATE SHIP THREE: *The pirate ship comes back around. The scene is exactly the same as it was before, except Lucy is there and the pirates are dancing a jig. The group are hopeful that the revolve will stop this time. It doesn't stop.*

NURSERY THREE: *All the cast on the ship, except Chris and Lucy, move into the nursery. They fall over and land in a pile on top of each other. Trevor is still kneeling at the fuse box.*

FOREST THREE: *Sandra and Annie are shouting at Jonathan. Sandra hits Jonathan with a bindle. Jonathan tries to kiss Sandra, but she pushes him away. Sandra and Annie throw Jonathan headfirst into the picnic table. Robert, Max, Dennis and Francis dance across the stage in front of the revolve and disappear into the wings.*

PIRATE SHIP FOUR: *Chris is now the only pirate on the* Jolly Roger. *He sings and dances with enthusiasm, trying to create a full scene by himself. As he jumps on the deck, Lucy rolls down the ship in her wheelchair and collides feetfirst with one of the balusters and gets stuck. As the pirate ship continues to revolve, we can see Chris kicking at Lucy's injured foot, trying to wheel her back to the top of the deck. Chris kicks it until it becomes dislodged (offstage).*

NURSERY FOUR: *Trevor, Francis, Robert, Max and Dennis are having an argument over the fuse box. They realise they have been seen, so they form the image of a pirate ship, using discarded props and bits of set from the nursery.*

As they step off the revolve, two ASMs run onstage with the blue sheet from the lagoon to create the sea. Trevor abandons the fuse box and runs offstage and into the wings.*

FOREST FOUR: *Jonathan is still being beaten by Annie and Sandra. The makeshift ship image breaks apart and various arguments break out.*

* If you do not have two available assistant stage managers in your production, other members of the cast can do this.

PIRATE SHIP FIVE: As the pirate ship comes around again, the cast frantically pile back onboard as Trevor wedges the broom in the side of the revolve so it stops turning. As the music ends, the cast strike a dramatic tableau and Max raises the flag of the Jolly Roger. *The broom budges and bends under the strain.*

CHRIS. How still the night is. Nothing sounds alive.

The car horn sound effect is played again.

A CAB!! Why is there a cab in the sea?! Revenge will soon be mine.

The car horn sound effect is played again.

COME ON!

ROBERT'S VOICE. Audition tape seventy-two. Arrogant man. Oh, I'm Chris Bean. I'm directing a play and playing Captain Hook at the same time. I have the cold, thin hands of a lizard.

Recording cuts out. Lucy peers at Chris' hands. Chris looks at Robert.

CHRIS. Quiet, you dogs, or I'll cast anchor in you! Now, you blithering scurs, you have to make your choice. Will you join my crew? Or will you die tonight in the light of the full moon?

The cast gesture U.S. R. *to where the moon should be. An unseen crew member awkwardly holds the moon up from behind the set* S. L. *The cast all change and gesture to the correct place where the moon is.*

SANDRA. We shall none of us ever be pirates.

CHRIS. Is that so, my dear, it'll be the plank for you, then. Eh, Smee?

DENNIS. *(Dressed as John.)* Aye, Captain!

Radio feedback sound.

Dennis, you're wearing the wrong costume. No, don't say that, that is obviously not a line. You are the worst actor I have ever worked with. I'm leaving. No, Carol, don't go. Gerry, I'm forty-two. I'm wasting my life working with these people. Carol, if you walk out of that door now you're not just walking away from this production, you are walking away from our marriage. This is a sham of a marriage, Gerry. I know it. You know it. Even the kids know it. Goodbye. She's gone. She's gone. ARGHHHH! ARGHHH! Thirteen years of marriage down the toilet. Keep it together, Gerry. It looks like you are going to have to step in and save yet another production. Hi, Dennis. How's it going, little guy? I'm going to be stepping in feeding you the lines, so we're going to pick up from "Aye, Captain" on the count of three, OK. One. Two. Three. Aye, Captain!

Dennis turns and blankly stares at Chris.

CHRIS. Get the plank ready, Mr Cecco.

FRANCIS. Aye, Sir!

Francis jumps down from the mast. They hit the deck a little hard, causing the ship to tip forwards and the whole cast to roll to the bottom.

CHRIS. Bring the first prisoner to the plank!

ROBERT. Aye!

SANDRA. Be brave, Tootles!

Everyone looks unsurely at Lucy.

ROBERT. Tootles, Captain?

CHRIS. ...Tootles.

Robert, Sandra, Francis and Dennis slowly push Lucy in the wheelchair up towards the plank. She rolls back down.

Walk to the end and meet your fate, vile child!

They slowly climb up the titled ship and gently push the wheelchair. They end up going too far and send the ship tipping in the other direction. The sudden shift in direction catapults Lucy off the ship. Trevor runs on D.S. *last minute and catches her. Trevor exits with Lucy in his arms, taking the wheelchair with him.*

There's none can save him now!

JONATHAN. *(Off.)* There is one!

Suddenly, Jonathan swings in on his wire. He lands on the front of the ship, tipping it back the other way. The cast tumble down it again.*

I'm coming to save you all.

* See page 74 for nonflying alternatives.

CHRIS. Pan!

SANDRA. Peter!

CHRIS. Surround them. This one's mine.

JONATHAN. Hook! The crocodile is here; he knows your end is near.

A ticking clock is heard and Max (as Crocodile), in the crocodile costume, enters from the S. L. *side and prowls around outside the ship.*

Dark and sinister man. Have at thee.*

PIRATE SHIP ONE: *The pairs begin their fight with three clear "en garde" moments. Sandra and Robert are* S. R., *Chris and Jonathan are centre, and Dennis and Francis fight Annie* S. L. *Annie doesn't have a sword, so she pulls out the broom to use as a sword. The revolve starts back up.*

NURSERY ONE: *The cast make their way into the nursery. They stop fighting so that they can focus on getting to the next moment of blocking and keep in line with the audience. They crowd Trevor—he pushes them all away and reveals that he is working on the electrics beneath the trap door.*

*Again—there are three clear "en garde" moments—*S. R., *centre, and then* S. L. *As Chris attempts to engage with Jonathan, he falls off the ladder and onto the bed. As he does so, he pulls down the framed painting of the London skyline, which swings (on hinges) and knocks Annie to the ground.*

FOREST ONE: *Chris runs into the forest, attempting to keep his fight going with Jonathan. Lucy is on the tree stairs, being tended to by Gill (now a paramedic).*

Chris gets up on the table and is hit in the crotch by the plank. He drops his hook.

Chris pushes the paramedic out of the way and goes up the stairs, taking Lucy's crutch as a weapon.

Dennis tries to stop the set going around by pushing against the tree. It carries on, taking him with it.

* See page 71 for an alternate revolve scene for 2D staging.

PIRATE SHIP TWO: *Chris and Robert debate on how to fix the tilting ship. Chris still has Lucy's crutch as a sword. On the final tilt, the backdrop falls down to reveal the poster for* Rapunzel, *featuring Sandra with very short hair, standing in front of a bungalow.*

NURSERY TWO: *Chris stands in the window and throws the crutch into the room. It hits Trevor. Trevor falls backwards and activates the pyro. Sandra is by the door, shouting at Trevor to fix the revolve. Jonathan hovers on the fly line above them.** *Sandra tries to pull him down by grabbing his legs, but he flies higher into the air and his trousers come away in her hands. The fuse box sparks and the revolve speeds up.*

FOREST TWO: *Chris goes into the forest, now sprinting quickly. Dennis is revealed. He is stuck to the main tree by the sheer speed of the revolve. Chris continues through the tree stairs and into the ship.*

PIRATE SHIP THREE: *Chris tilts the stage and Robert slides down the rail of the ship, hitting his crotch. Chris continues to charge around the revolve to stay* C. S.

NURSERY THREE: *Chris opens the door and hits Sandra. Trevor tries to catch her.*

FOREST THREE: *Chris continues with the same track through the forest and up the tree stairs. Dennis' costume is stuck to the main tree, but he is not in it.*

PIRATE SHIP FOUR: *Chris slides down the deck past Max, who smiles sweetly.*

NURSERY FOUR: *Chris goes through the door again, knocking out Sandra once more. Trevor throws a large sheaf of "stage revolve instruction" papers up in the air. Dennis runs, semi-naked, across the front of the stage and exits. Chris tries to exit the nursery, but Lucy opens the door from the other side, and it hits him in the face, knocking him to the ground.*

* See page 74 for nonflying alternatives.

FOREST FOUR: *As we move into the forest, Robert is seen clinging to the revolve, dragging along at floor level. Annie begins to tape the set with "Do Not Cross" tape.*

PIRATE SHIP FIVE: *Max waves at the audience and smiles, having a great time.*

NURSERY FIVE: *Trevor hits the fuse box and sparks fly once again. Dennis jumps back onto the set, back in costume, fastening his buttons. He cowers in the bottom bunk of the bed.*

FOREST FIVE: *Gill/Paramedic injects herself and passes out.*

PIRATE SHIP SIX: *Robert, runs on from* D.S. L. *He's on fire, and Trevor extinguishes him. As the fire is put out, all the cast run on from different directions to try to get into the nursery.*

NURSERY SIX: *We end in the nursery as the set grinds to a halt. Jonathan falls from the rig/window, hurtling towards Sandra. Max dives towards Sandra and pushes her out of the way.*[*]

SANDRA. You saved me…Peter. You're a hero.

Max pulls off the head of his crocodile costume.

MAX. I'm not Peter. I'm the crocodile.

Francis crawls towards the D.S. R. *area. Suddenly, the chair shoots out and hits them in the head. They fall unconscious. The cast audibly moan. Chris slumps to the floor, broken and sobbing. Lucy hobbles unsurely towards the chair, discarding her crutches on the way. Slowly, she picks up the narrator's storybook. The lights dim and a spotlight comes up.*

LUCY. T…Thus…perished James Hook and his crew, devoured by the merciless jaws of the crocodile. Wendy, of course, had stood, taking no part in the fight, though now she watched her hero with glistening eyes, and when he slept that night she held him tight…

Sandra kisses Max. Music begins.

* See page 74 for nonflying alternatives.

JONATHAN. Cast off, me hearties! Hoist the sails and let us go home! Obey the orders of Captain Pan!

LUCY. …and now sadly it is time to bring an end to our tale, for we must leave Neverland…

Annie (as Tinker Bell) stands with Jonathan by the ship.

…where Peter and Tinker Bell sailed the *Jolly Roger* across the skies and were to have many more adventures.

Jonathan, Annie, Robert and Chris exit.

Curly returned to the Lost Boys and scared them with another story of Marooners' Rock.

Annie (as Curly) crosses the stage, now dressed as Curly and quickly exits.

But now we must return to that desolate home from which three of our characters had taken heartless flight so long ago.

Dennis, Sandra, Max and Trevor gather at the side of the revolve and push it around to fully reveal the nursery again. They then exit behind the nursery. Annie runs on as Lisa.

Lisa, sat by the window, and seeing the children approach, ran to fetch her mistress.

Annie rushes out through the nursery door and immediately reenters as Mrs Darling.

Mrs Darling looked out at her children and the smile at the corner of her mouth that had withered with grief, brightened.

Wendy, John and…the crocodile, found the window open.

Sandra, Dennis, and Max enter through the window. Max helps Sandra.

On seeing them, Mrs Darling could scarcely speak, such was the emotion that overwhelmed her delicate heart. Mr Darling came rushing in from the yard to celebrate the homecoming of his dear ones.

Chris enters dressed as Mr Darling, but he is still wearing his hook. He embraces the children. Annie, Sandra, Max, Dennis and Chris create a tableau C. S.

And as for the Lost Boys, they were all adopted by the Darlings and, for the first time, felt the love of a mother. There could not have been a lovelier sight, but there was none to see it, except a strange boy who was sitting at the window.

Snow falls gently outside the nursery. Jonathan, nicely silhouetted, looks in from the window. Music begins to play.

A ladder appears in the window and Robert climbs up, dressed as the shadow. He leans on the windowsill behind Peter.

Eventually, they would all grow up. Their adventures with Peter Pan and Neverland would become the shadows of memories, and it wouldn't take long for them to forget how to fly, even to chase their hats and of course they would soon cease to believe in fairies. But right now, the children, Mr and Mrs Darling...and the crocodile stood together, united in their newfound bliss, and perhaps it was at this moment they all realised that to live would be an awfully big adventure.

Music swells. Lights fade to black.

Lights come back up for a reprise of "The World of Make Believe."

ALL. With give and take then you can make,
Whatever you can conceive,
With faith and trust and fairy dust,
And the world of make believe
And the world of make believe.

End of Play

APPENDIX

Neverland Tree Drop Alt

(No tree costume)

JONATHAN. Wendy, look. We're here!

Annie switches on her fairy lights, and we hear an electrical clunk. All the lights immediately go out, plunging the stage into darkness.

Beat.

SANDRA. Oh, Peter, it's beautiful.

JONATHAN. You can see all of Neverland from here, Wendy.

Trevor enters in the darkness and gives a torch to Sandra, which she shines onto her face.

SANDRA. I've never seen trees quite like these before.

Sandra shines the torch onto the stage to highlight the set, but she accidentally shines it on Trevor, who is in a precarious position, trying to pass a torch to Jonathan. They are both startled.

SANDRA and TREVOR. Argh!

SANDRA. Peter, who is that?

JONATHAN. That, Wendy, is Tootles, one of the Lost Boys.

Sandra moves the torch and shines it on Lucy, who looks terrified.

LUCY. *(Totally terrified.)* I'm…Tootles.

JONATHAN. That, Wendy, is Tootles, one of the Lost Boys. The other one was a…err a mermaid.

The torch shines back onto Trevor who, after a beat, does an impression of a mermaid. Suddenly the lights snap back on and Trevor leaves, taking the torches.

Hello, Tootles! What news?

Lucy stares in silence at the audience. She tries to run off, but Robert appears from the back of the forest and pushes her back on.

ROBERT. Lucy. You're doing this.

Lucy tries to speak, but her nerves get the better of her.

LUCY. Pe… Pe…

Robert hides behind the large tree at the back of the set. He leans in and prompts her.

ROBERT. Peter.

LUCY. I…tell you have something. No! I Peter, tell you something have.

ROBERT. I have to tell you something!

JONATHAN. Oh yes? What is it you want to tell me, Tootles?

LUCY. Hooktin Cap…Captain Cook…Hook capped Curly.

ROBERT. *(In a boy's voice.)* Captain Hook's kidnapped Curly.

LUCY. We have to, we to have, we…

Lucy looks on terrified.

ROBERT. We have to rescue him. For God's sake.

Robert hits the back of the tree in frustration, and a large heavy branch falls on Lucy with a thump, crushing her leg and taking her out of view. We hear a muffled scream from Lucy. Robert exits sheepishly.

JONATHAN. You're right, Tootles. Tinker Bell, go and find where they've taken him

Annie ducks behind a tree. The Tinker Bell light reemerges and they all watch it fly off. Annie is then seen as she gets up and exits from behind the tree.

Panpipe music suddenly plays. Jonathan quickly gets out his panpipes to mime playing them, but he is too late and the music stops.

SANDRA. Oh, Peter! You play beautifully…

Suddenly, we hear Chris, Robert and Dennis singing and growling.

JONATHAN. Pirates! Quickly, into the hideout.

Revolve Sequence
(2D set version)

JONATHAN. Dark and sinister man. Have at thee.

***PIRATE SHIP ONE:** The pairs begin their fight with three clear "en garde" moments. Sandra and Robert are* S. R.*, Chris and Jonathan are centre, and Dennis and Francis fight Annie* S. L. *Annie doesn't have a sword, so she pulls out the broom to use as a sword. The revolve starts back up.*

***NURSERY ONE:** The cast make their way into the nursery. They stop fighting so that they can focus on getting to the next moment of blocking and keep in line with the audience. They crowd Trevor—he pushes them all away and reveals that he is working on the electrics beneath the trap door.*

*Again—there are three clear "en garde" moments—*S. R.*, centre, and then* S. L. *As Chris attempts to engage with Jonathan, he falls off the ladder and onto the bed. As he does so, he pulls down the hinged sunflower picture, and it swings down to knock Annie to the ground.*

***FOREST ONE:** Chris runs into the forest, attempting to keep his fight going with Jonathan. Lucy is on the tree stairs, being tended to by Gill (now a paramedic).*

Chris gets up on the table and is hit in the crotch by the plank. He drops his hook.

Chris pushes the paramedic out of the way and goes up the stairs, taking Lucy's crutch as a weapon.

Dennis tries to stop the set going around by pushing against the tree but can't get the revolve to stop.

***PIRATE SHIP TWO:** Chris and Robert debate on how to fix the tilting ship. Chris still has Lucy's crutch as a sword. On the final tilt, the backdrop falls down to reveal the poster for* Rapunzel, *featuring Sandra with very short hair, standing in front of a bungalow.*

NURSERY TWO: *Chris stands in the window and throws his crutch into the room. It hits Trevor. Trevor falls backwards and activates the pyro. Sandra is by the door, shouting at Trevor to fix the revolve. Jonathan hovers on the fly line above them. Sandra tries to pull him down by grabbing his legs, but he flies higher into the air and his trousers come away in her hands. The fuse box sparks and the revolve speeds up.*

FOREST TWO: *Chris goes into the forest. Dennis tries to stop the revolve by using the mallet from the top of the show. Chris continues through the tree stairs and onto the ship.*

PIRATE SHIP THREE: *Chris tilts the stage and Robert slides down the rail of the ship, hitting his crotch. Chris continues to charge around the revolve to stay* C. S.

NURSERY THREE: *Chris opens the door and hits Sandra. Trevor tries to catch her.*

FOREST THREE: *Chris continues with the same track through the forest and up the tree stairs.*

PIRATE SHIP FOUR: *Chris slides down the deck past Max, who smiles sweetly.*

NURSERY FOUR: *Chris goes through the door again, knocking out Sandra once more. Trevor throws a large sheaf of "stage revolve instruction" papers up in the air. Dennis tries to stop the revolve, this time with a sea horse from the UV scene. Chris tries to exit the nursery, but, this time, the door is opened from the other side, and he is knocked out.*

FOREST FOUR: *As we move into the forest, Robert is seen clinging to the revolve, dragging along at floor level. Annie begins to tape the set with "Do Not Cross" tape.*

PIRATE SHIP FIVE: *Max waves at the audience and smiles, having a great time.*

NURSERY FIVE: *Trevor hits the fuse box and sparks fly* *once again. Dennis jumps back onto the set, back in costume, fastening his buttons. He cowers in the bottom bunk of the bed.*

FOREST FIVE: *Gill/Paramedic injects herself and passes out.*

PIRATE SHIP SIX: *Robert, runs on from* D.S. L. *He's on fire, and Trevor extinguishes him. As the fire is put out, all the cast run on from different directions to try to get into the nursery.*

NURSERY SIX: *We end in the nursery as the set grinds to a halt. Jonathan falls from the rig/window, hurtling towards Sandra. Max dives towards Sandra and pushes her out of the way.*

SANDRA. You saved me… Peter. You're a hero.

Nonflying Alternatives

We want to make sure the show is possible to mount without flying or with reduced flying.

We're are open to individual productions finding their own creative solutions to do this, but we've listed an alternative for each point where flying appears in the stage directions that will allow the action to flow and the scene to function.

Pg. 24. Jonathan can simply enter from D.S. R. for his entrance as Peter Pan. Another option is that he can climb through the window and down the bed that Max and Dennis are trapped in whilst Sandra lies on the top bunk, doing her best to ignore him and pretend to be asleep.

Pg. 27. Jonathan can run up the bed and Robert tries to follow.

Pg. 28. Jonathan can climb down off the bed, knocking Robert off the window ledge.

Pg. 30. Jonathan can climb out of the window and plummet to the ground.

Pg. 43. The fight with Chris can take place without flying. Then, at the end of the fight, rather than Jonathan flying up into the rig, he can be pushed back by Chris into one of the tall rocks, causing them to fall on top of Jonathan and knock him out.

Pg. 49–51. Trevor can play Peter Pan without flying. He can enter from U.S. R. into the forest. The jokes where he reads incorrectly from the script still function, and he's still knocked out by climbing onto the picnic table. The dialogue before this point could be easily truncated, and he wouldn't shout off to stage management. Once unconscious, Robert would drag Trevor offstage before returning to try and play Peter Pan himself.

Pg. 63. Jonathan can just simply run on from D.S. L. and climb up onto the Jolly Roger.

Pg. 65. Jonathan can fight Chris on the Jolly Roger and join him in trying to run against the revolve in an attempt to stay in view of the audience.

Pg. 66. The action where Jonathan plummets towards Sandra can be altered so that it's a falling piece of set that Max saves her from.

Music and Third-Party Materials Use Note

A license to produce PETER PAN GOES WRONG does not include a performance license for any third-party or copyrighted music. For "Yo Ho," "Lullaby," and "World of Make Believe," licensees should create an original composition or use music in the public domain.

Licensees are solely responsible for obtaining formal written permission from copyright owners to use copyrighted music and/or other copyrighted third-party materials (e.g. artworks, logos) in the performance of this play and are strongly cautioned to do so. If no such permission is obtained by the licensee, then the licensee must use only original music and materials that the licensee owns and controls. Licensees are solely responsible and liable for clearances of all third-party copyrighted materials, including without limitation music, and shall indemnify the copyright owners of the play(s) and their licensing agent, Dramatists Play Service, an imprint of Concord Theatricals Corp., against any costs, expenses, losses and liabilities arising from the use of such copyrighted third-party materials by licensees. For music, please contact the appropriate music licensing authority in your territory for the rights to any incidental music.

About Mischief

Mischief creates award-winning comedy for stage, screen and beyond, with long-running shows continuously playing in both New York and London, as well as regular tours across the USA, Canada, and the UK. Now a global sensation, they are currently bringing joy and laughter to audiences around the world.

Discover more mischief at mischiefcomedy.com

Follow us and be social @mischiefcomedy

THE PLAY THAT GOES WRONG

THE COMEDY ABOUT A BANK ROBBERY

PETER PAN GOES WRONG

MISCHIEF MOVIE NIGHT

MAGIC GOES WRONG

GROAN UPS

THE GOES WRONG SHOW

MISCHIEF MAKERS

THE NATIVITY GOES WRONG

CHRISTMAS CAROL GOES WRONG

For Mischief Worldwide Ltd

Directors .... Mark Bentley, Jonathan Burke, Jo Danvers, Henry Lewis, Hilary Strong (Chair) Kenny Wax
CEO .... Jo Danvers
Head of Marketing & Brand .... Harry Lockyear
Licensing Manager .... Jessica Hall
Interim Licensing Manager (Job Share) .... Kezia Lockhouse
Marketing Coordinator .... Nathan Garwood
Executive Assistant .... Dorothy Oehmler
Consultant Financial Director .... Charlotte Johnson
Bookkeeper .... Jai Tosniwal
Literary Rights .... Nicki Stoddart for United Agents Ltd.

Additional Copyright Information

The right to recreate the West End and Broadway productions of PETER PAN GOES WRONG and/or to promote a production on the basis that it is a version of those productions is expressly reserved to the owners of the copyright and trademark-protected contributions to those productions and their advertising, specifically:

Directions: © 2013 Adam Meggido
Set Design: © 2013 Simon Scullion
Lighting Design: © 2013 Matt Haskins
Costume Design: © 2013 Roberto Surace
Sound Design: © 2013 Ella Wahlström
Original Compositions: © 2013 Rob Falconer & Richard Baker

and any incorporation of material elements of such contributions in a production given under this license and without a separate license to incorporate such contributions is a breach of this license and of copyright law.

Advertising and promotion of a production given under this license in a way which suggests to the public a connection with or that the production concerned is a version of the West End and/or Broadway production by incorporating the Falling G Logo or other material elements of those productions' publicity which may reasonably be expected to create this suggestion in the public mind is a breach of trademark and/or other applicable law.

All such breaches are strictly forbidden under this license.

If in doubt as to whether what you intend to do may be a breach of the above provisions you must contact Concord Theatricals before disseminating the doubtful matters to the public in advertising or production.

Notice to Professional Licensees Interested in Presenting a Version of the Broadway and West End Production of the Play

Without prejudice to the notice on the previous page, the above rights and digital and physical resources to realise the contributions are available on a basis to suit a wide variety of production capabilities of professional licensees of the Play upon application to Mischief Worldwide Ltd. at info@mischiefworldwide.com.